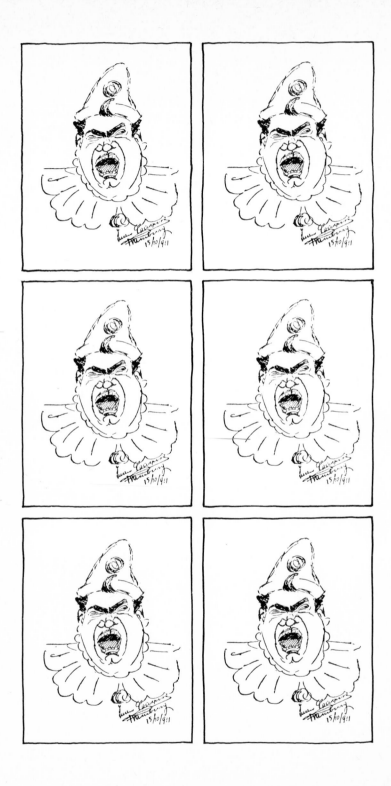

# The performing world of the singer

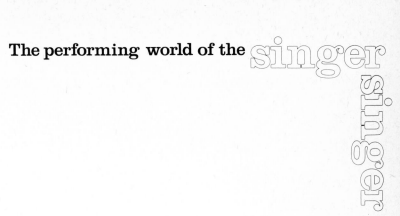

The performing world of the

# singer

Alan Blackwood

with a profile of
Sherrill Milnes

singer

Silver Burdett Company

Designed and produced by Breslich & Foss, London

Design: Leslie & Lorraine Gerry
Picture Research: Mary Corcoran
House Editor: Timothy Roberts
Interview with Sherrill Milnes: Frank Granville Barker
Interview with Terri Balash: Deborah Waroff
Interview with Matthew Best: Nicholas Robinson

© Breslich & Foss

Published in the United States
by Silver Burdett Conmpany, © 1981

Library of Congress Catalog Card Number: 8150296
ISBN 0-382-06591-3

Filmset and printed in Great Britain by
BAS Printers Limited

# Contents

# Ten Centuries of Song

# 1

## Lost Roots

Singing is both natural and spontaneous. From earliest times laments for the dead, odes to the living, and shouted choruses of triumph or anger, have welled up from the hearts and throats of men and women. Prehistoric cave paintings show figures dancing and playing simple instruments, and we can be certain they sang as well. These paintings are mostly to do with hunting, and many of their songs probably described their constant search for food as they struggled for survival. Much further on, about 5000 B.C., the Egyptians represented in their wall paintings people playing harps and flutes, and we know that music was very important to early Greek drama. Sadly, however, there are few clues to the sounds and rhythms created, and the true origins of singing are mostly lost to us.

## From One Voice to Many

Nevertheless we have a link with the past in the traditional chant of the Jewish synagogues which goes right back to Old Testament times. This style of chant was carried over into the earliest forms of Christian worship, and this tradition was in turn revised to form *plainsong*. Plainsong was used in the recitation of the church liturgy and was sung by choirs of men in unison (everybody singing the same note). It followed the stress of the words being sung,

1

A group of young Egyptian musicians painted on the wall of a tomb at Thebes. If only we knew exactly how they sang and danced!

and so had no real rhythm of its own. The men who sang it were mostly monks; and while others in the monastery tilled the fields, cooked the food, looked after the sick and needy, it was their duty to sing the plainsong chants and responses for all the services and other religious observances that went on virtually round the clock. Such music would soon have become second nature to them. It has a kind of rarified, timeless beauty to our modern ears. It probably meant rather less to those dragged from their medieval beds upon a cold winter's dawn, to stand wrapped and shivering in their habits, trying to raise sleepy voices in praise of God.

2

This 'Guidonian Hand' comes from a medieval manuscript. It illustrates a method developed by Guido of Arezzo, a Benedictine monk, to help choirs learn music

Gradually the plainsong developed into something more complicated, and in the interests of musical variety the different melodic lines began to move up and down independently of each other. In order to remember these increasingly tricky melodies a Benedictine monk named Guido of Arezzo developed a system of musical notation which allowed him to write down the notes. One memory aid he devised related notes to different segments of the fingers. By holding one hand open and using the index finger of the other as a pointer, he could help to lead his singers through a new piece of music. This kind of part-singing grew into the style of music we

3

know as *polyphony*—a word taken from the Greek, meaning 'many sounds'.

## Wandering Minstrels

The story of singing and of song, as it has come down to us from ages past, is by no means confined to religion as we can see from the words of one medieval song:

In the public house to die
Is my resolution;
Let wine to my lips be nigh
At life's dissolution.

Songs expressing such bawdy sentiments as these were performed by groups called *goliards*—often young students who were what we might now call drop-outs from the monasteries and other places of learning. Other songs sprang from the lips of *jongleurs*—the French name for sometimes highly skilled and versatile singers, musicians and acrobats who entertained the crowds at festivals. Nobody can be sure exactly what their singing was like. Far more is known about the music of the troubadours and other minstrel-knights of the Middle Ages. The word troubadour comes from old Provençal and means 'finder', inventor of poems and melodies; and it was in Provence, in southern France, that the troubadours flourished. Many of them were kings and princes who had fought in one or other of the crusades, and their music was influenced by their years in the Holy Land (now in Syria, Israel, Lebanon and Jordan). Their melodies often had a plaintive, Arabic sound, and were accompanied on instruments like the rebec, a string instrument that also came from the Middle East. Noblemen practised music for its own sake; but the poorer musicians relied for food and shelter, and perhaps for money also, on entertaining the nobility in their castles.

Elsewhere in France there were similar minstrel-knights called *trouvères*; in Germany, *minnesingers* ('singers of love'); in England, bards and minstrels, some of their traditions going back to pre-Roman times. Richard the Lionheart was a crusader knight also renowned as a minstrel. There is a story that when he was held captive to ransom, his old minstrel

4

Die krieget mit sange k̄ walth' von voglweior · h̄ wolfran von Eschilbach.
h̄ Rennauder alte der tugenthafte Schriber hemrich vō Ofterungē
vij klingesoz von Vngerlant.

A 14th-century illustration showing minnesingers, including the famous Walter von der Vogelweide, gathered at the hill-top castle of Wartburg for a song contest. These legendary events inspired Wagner's opera *Tannhäuser*

companion Blondel de Nesles wandered from castle to castle singing a song they had composed together, until Richard eventually heard him and sang out in reply from behind his prison wall. This is probably a legend, but it conveys the romantic atmosphere created by these poet-musicians with their songs of valour in distant lands, and of chivalrous love for ladies whom they swore to defend with their honour and their life. A big feature of life among these various minstrels was their contests of poetry and song. In Britain these gatherings of bards who listened to each other's song and elected champion poets and musicians, have survived to this day in the Welsh Eisteddfod festivals.

The winners of a Welsh Eisteddfod of poetry and song, about seventy years ago. Despite appearances, they have been taking it all very seriously

The social standing of musicians generally—and that primarily meant singers—was high during the later Middle Ages and into the Renaissance period. Henry V of England may have composed what is known as the Agincourt Song, a quite difficult piece in several parts, celebrating his victory over the French in 1415. Even if he was not actually the composer, he almost certainly led his troops in singing it, showing the importance he attached to music in the make-up of a king. The Battle of Agincourt was a landmark in the Hundred Years War, the long drawn-out struggle between the royal houses of England and France. But while the soldiers fought each other, scholars, poets and musicians of whatever nationality were welcomed wherever they went, and often moved in the highest circles. If you were a trained singer and scholar in the fifteenth century you might well have been attracted to the rich and powerful province of Burgundy in eastern France, where Duke Philip the Good held court. While playing off the English against the French in war, he lavished money on the arts and music. At one truly fantastic feast, intended to launch a new crusade, singers played a big part in the accompanying spectacle. At the climax an elephant was led into the banqueting hall, and on its back was a model castle containing the figure of a woman. In fact, the 'woman' was a man, who then sang in a falsetto voice, pleading for help from the assembled company. Among the singers employed by Philip were the famous composers Binchois and Dufay.

## The Renaissance

The Renaissance, or 'rebirth', was a period during the fifteenth and sixteenth centuries, of tremendous expansion in science and in the arts. It was the age of Galileo, Magellan and Columbus, of Leonardo da Vinci, Michelangelo and Shakespeare. It was also the period when singing enjoyed what we might truly call its golden age. The growth of polyphony led to choral music of increasing complexity and beauty. Composers and choristers such as Jean de Ockeghem, Josquin des Prés and Roland de Lassus all contributed to the process of weaving lines of melody into richer and richer patterns of sound, both in their

Jean de Ockeghem, one of the great Netherlands composers of polyphonic choral music, pictured among a group of singers

religious music and in their secular (non-religious) *chansons* and other songs. Just how complex such music could become is shown by a motet (sacred hymn) called *Spem in alium* by the English composer Thomas Tallis, who lived during the reigns of Henry VIII and Elizabeth I; it is written in forty individual parts, and produces a great wash of sound. Some music of the time was much simpler, though, largely because church authorities had objected to the fact that the words were often inaudible. Pierluigi da Palestrina, a choirboy and then a choirmaster in Rome, is famous for his pure-sounding choral music in this new spirit; in fact, there is a legend that his *Missa Papae Marcelli* (Mass

7

A contemporary print of Palestrina presenting one of his compositions to the Pope. Although he continued to write religious music, Palestrina abandoned his plans to become a priest, married and became a shrewd property investor

for Pope Marcellus) was all that saved music from being banned entirely by the Catholic Church!

Meanwhile, in Elizabethan England there was a craze for singing madrigals, part-songs for small groups of singers. The madrigal originated in Italy and spread to England in 1588, year of the Spanish Armada; and soon there was a whole generation of English madrigal composers, notably Thomas Morley, Thomas Weelkes, John Wilbye and Orlando Gibbons. Their songs of love, joy or a kind of gentle melancholy were learnt by the nobility at court and well-to-do ladies and gentlemen in their country estates, where music was still eagerly cultivated. The most famous collection of madrigals was called *The Triumphs of Oriana*, the name 'Oriana' fancifully referring to Queen Elizabeth herself. Music like this was published in 'partbooks', each book containing music for only one voice (soprano, alto and so on). It was necessary for the singer to count very carefully since once he got lost there was no way of knowing where everyone else had got to! Only in the last two centuries has music commonly been printed in score format (with all the parts shown together).

In Renaissance Germany, people were singing a very different kind of music. Martin Luther, a German priest, had attacked the Church of Rome for corrupt practices and then established the new Protestant Church. This was the Reformation, and it led to two hundred years of conflict and bloodshed between Protestants and Roman Catholics. But Luther himself was no kill-joy. He wanted singing to play a more personal role in services. In the Church of Rome trained professional choirs sang the magnificent polyphonic masses and motets—not the kind of music congregations could participate in. In their place Luther introduced strong and sturdy hymn tunes called chorales, set to German words instead of high-flown Latin, and which ordinary people could sing together. He often used secular melodies in church, saying, 'why should the Devil have all the best tunes?' From that time to the present day Protestant congregations have raised their voices in the singing of chorales—or hymns, as we call them. Some of our best-loved Christmas carols—like 'While shepherds watched'—were composed in the early days of the Protestant Church.

## Early Opera

Opera is one of the most varied, colourful, exciting and extravagant of all the performing arts. It began at the very end of the Renaissance and initiated what we call the Baroque era of music. It grew logically out of the aims of the Renaissance, which was preoccupied with the revival of the culture of Ancient Greece and Rome. A group of earnest Italians calling themselves the Camerata ('Fellowship') met in Florence to try and revive Ancient Greek drama. They knew little about its style but believed that it had been all sung; and they accordingly devised a new style of music suitable for plays set entirely to music. The polyphonic style was thought too complex—particularly as it was of the utmost importance that the *words* should not only be heard but also matched by music that followed their

A famous portrait of Monteverdi, who was Director of Music at St Mark's, Venice. The plan and acoustics of the Church inspired him and other composers to develop a very dramatic kind of choral music, in which different groups of singers answered each other from various parts of the building

emotional meaning. The style that was born has survived to the present day—the *recitative*. In this style the singer is able to declaim the words and music freely against a simple accompaniment of chords. Here for the first time was a style of vocal music which, unlike polyphony, would be meaningless if played by instruments. Furthermore, it introduced the idea of 'solo' and 'accompaniment'. Such music gave the singer a new status and charisma in the musical world.

Around 1600 the earliest operas were written, entirely in recitative, and very dull they were too. It took a composer of genius to bring real musical interest and dramatic life to opera; and that composer was Claudio Monteverdi. He wrote operas for the Duke of Mantua (including *Orfeo*) and later at Venice where the first public opera house opened in 1637. He introduced greater variety into the singing roles, including song-like pieces ('arias') as well as recitative and using the instruments in an imaginative way to highlight the stage action. His last opera—written at the ripe old age of seventy-five—was *The Coronation of Poppea* and, rather than the remote Greek gods and goddesses of earlier operas, it deals in a very lifelike way with the passionate human feelings of men and women at the court of the Roman emperor Nero. For that reason this is one of the very few early operas that has entered the regular repertory of modern opera-houses.

For while Monteverdi was writing such advanced works as *Poppea*, other composers were writing operas that depended more on stage spectacle and virtuoso singing than on the plot or the characters' feelings. Such lavish entertainments were far from the ideals of the Florence Camerata—but opera had become a public art form, and the public wanted entertainment above all. One opera, *The Golden Apple* by Pietro Cesti, had twenty stage sets, over sixty scenes and several ballet sequences. Every technical device of the time was used to create sensational stage effects. Winches and pulleys moved large chunks of scenery to and fro across the stage, or transported gods and goddesses through the air. And as the grand climax the scenery itself might be designed to collapse or go up in smoke and flames. (Very often such spectacles got out of control, and most Baroque opera houses seem to have burned down eventually!)

Such extravagances were much enjoyed by royalty, nowhere more so than at the French court at Versailles where Louis XIV, most powerful monarch of the age, had built his great palace. 'The Sun King', as he was called, and his court sat in splendour, while the ornate opera-ballets of Jean Baptiste Lully were staged for their private pleasure. Even the orchestra might be divided in two, to provide Louis with an uninterrupted view of the proceedings. Such operas were entirely devoted to the glorification of the king, and allowed little in the way of drama or realism.

11

A contemporary illustration to one of Lully's opera-ballets— the 'movie-spectaculars' of their day

The orchestral overtures (from the French *ouverture*, or 'opening') that Lully wrote accompanied the stately arrival of Louis XIV and his court for the performance. But in Italy overtures written for public performances were intended more to bring rowdy and high-spirited audiences to order before the opera actually began—especially since there was no lowering of house lights before the invention of electricity. The days when overtures had some musical bearing on the opera to follow, and audiences might pay attention to them, were still a long way off.

Something a lot of people enjoyed doing was following the words during the performance. They could buy a pocket-sized edition of the text, called a *libretto* (the Italian for 'little book'). Later 'libretto' came to mean the actual text of an opera. Surviving examples of these seventeenth- and eighteenth-century librettos nearly all bear the marks of wax, since the audience could buy small candles to attach to their copies to help them with their reading.

While the French style of opera with elaborate ballet sequences flourished in France itself, the Italian *opera seria* became popular elsewhere in Europe, including London. That was where George Frideric Handel chose to seek his fortune, for it was becoming the richest European capital. German by birth, Handel travelled to Italy as a young man, and learned a good deal about opera there. The *opera seria*, or 'serious opera' that Handel later did so much to promote in London had several distinctive features. It nearly always showed some heroic or tragic episode from ancient history—though a happy end was usually called for, however improbable this made the plot. There were also special conventions about the way the arias should be sung and about how many arias should be given to each character. (Two of Handel's leading ladies once fought on stage over some such matter!) The singers were the centre of attention; they were the superstars of their day, highly paid and pampered, and often very tempera-

Handel directing a performance of one of his oratorios

mental. None of them cared much about the opera—
except when they were singing—and might well
wave or blow kisses from the stage to admirers they
noticed among the audience. But then the audience
also cared little for the plot; they would chat, eat
supper or pursue love affairs during the musically
uneventful recitatives, resuming their attention to
hear an aria sung by their favourite singer. These
arias were often wildly spectacular vocally. The first
section of each aria was usually repeated with
elaborate variations invented by the singers to show
off their technique. The poor composer often had to
hear his music murdered by the less skilled night-
ingales on stage. Handel, who seems to have had a
way with obstinate singers, was once trying to get a
tenor to sing an aria as he had composed it. The tenor
threatened to jump into the harpsichord if he was not
allowed his own way, to which Handel replied, 'Tell
me when, and I will advertise it; for the public would
sooner see you jump, than hear you sing.'

When we speak of someone being a 'prima donna',
we are harking back to the formidable figure of the
*prima donna* (or 'first lady') of *opera seria*, jealously
guarding her status and liable to throw a fit if
anything was done to upset her. Such ladies were
normally far above the humble composer in the
opera-house hierarchy; but seem to have met their
match in Handel. There is another story about his
trying to get his own way, with a prima donna this
time; grabbing the lady, and threatening to throw
her out of the window, he bellowed: 'Madame, I know
you are a true she devil, but I will show you that I am
Beelzebub, the chief devil!'

The opera house of those days must have been even
more exciting and colourful than that of today. It is
difficult to recreate that excitement when performing
Handel's operas today, because modern audiences
cannot accept the artificial conventions which even
Handel's superb music is unable to break through.
What is more, we have lost the vocal sounds of those
days because of the different techniques of voice
training—not to mention the (mostly fortunate) loss
of the most characteristic Baroque voice, the *castrato*.

Castrati were men who had been castrated as boys

14

A sketch of the famous castrato Farinelli during performance. The odd appearance of the man is probably no exaggeration, as castrati were often strange-looking people

in order to preserve their high-pitched voices. The church employed castrati because it did not allow women in choirs, but with the growth of opera many of the best castrati found fame and fortune on the stage. Their extraordinary tone—quite distinct from either boys or women—was one big attraction. Beyond that, they often grew very large, giving them a phenomenal lung power. They could hang on to a note for minutes on end, and other singers or wind players who tried to compete usually ended up gasping and blue in the face—triumphs for the castrati that always brought the house down. Most celebrated of these amazing singers was Carlo Broschi, known as Farinelli. He was fêted wherever he went, and women at the opera used to swoon when he started singing. He was summoned to the court of Philip V of Spain, where the king had sunk into a bad state of melancholy, and for ten years Farinelli sang the same songs to the sick monarch every night—the only person who could soothe his nerves and bring him sleep.

## Oratorio

London audiences eventually tired of the none-too-rational Italian opera, despite the beautiful music that Handel was writing. So the composer turned to oratorio, another musical form that had come from Italy. Oratorios were a kind of religious opera, but needed no scenery or costumes. They became popular in Italy and elsewhere because they gave audiences a chance to hear their favourite singers during Lent, when opera itself was forbidden. Handel's most famous oratorio is *Messiah*, first performed at a charity concert in Dublin in 1742. It was rapturously received from the start, and Handel lived out his remaining years almost as a British national hero.

How different was the life of Johann Sebastian Bach. After a number of court positions, he finally became Cantor, or choirmaster, at the church school of St Thomas in Leipzig. On arrival, he found the premises to be in a very tumbledown condition and the schoolboys neglected, undisciplined and poorly trained. Nevertheless, Bach was supposed to keep up a supply of choirboys to the city's many churches, and for St Thomas's Church itself to provide new music for every Sunday and festival of the church year. Bach's years in Leipzig were full of disagreements with the Council and many other strains and stresses in what was generally a tough and thankless job of work. Yet it was in those years that he wrote

most of his choral music, including a great many church cantatas (from the Italian *cantare*, 'to sing'), and two oratorio-type settings of the Easter story, or 'passions'. A surprising feature of all these works, which are very hard to sing, is that the soprano and alto solos were sung by boys, since women were not allowed to sing in church; yet their music is just as elaborate as that given to the tenor and bass. Presumably voices broke later then than now.

Bach's *St Matthew Passion* and *St John Passion* have solo parts for Christ himself, Pontius Pilate and other characters in the drama. The story is told by the Evangelist (a tenor) and there are recitatives, arias and choruses much as in a Baroque opera. There are also the familiar Lutheran chorales that give the music a solemnity rare in the more exuberant style of Handel's oratorios. The *St Matthew Passion* contains some of the most moving religious music for voices; but at its first performance it seems either to have made no impression upon the congregation, or to

J. S. Bach, seated at the keyboard and surrounded by his very large family. Twenty children by two marriages tied him to salaried posts, such as court composer, organist and choirmaster. Opera would have been too risky a venture for him

17

have created the wrong one. At a particularly dramatic moment, one worthy old lady, a pillar of Leipzig society, was heard to declare: 'God help us! It is, to be sure, a comic opera!'

## Later Choral Music

Handel and Bach, born in the same year (1685), and dead within ten years of each other, were the last two great composers to write large quantities of choral music. Much great music for chorus and soloists has been written since. We need only think of such masterpieces as Haydn's oratorio *The Creation*, Beethoven's immense *Missa Solemnis* ('Solemn Mass'), Verdi's *Requiem Mass* (a Mass in memory of the dead), Mahler's Eighth Symphony ('The Symphony of a Thousand') or Elgar's *The Dream of Gerontius*. But none of these composers is thought of as a specialist in big choral works. Where large-scale vocal music is concerned, most composers after Handel and Bach were more interested in opera.

## Comic Opera

During the eighteenth century, comic opera became very popular. Such opera dealt with the lives and feelings of ordinary men and women, the characters often being servants who are more witty than their masters. The first English comic opera was *The Beggar's Opera*, which presents a kind of topsy-turvy

William Hogarth's portrayal of a scene from *The Beggar's Opera*. In many of his other paintings, this artist depicted the same corrupt society that John Gay satirised in his opera

world where criminals such as highwaymen and receivers of stolen goods are shown as being superior, or at least equal, to aristocrats and politicians. Written by John Gay, it was not so much an opera as a play with songs (like the 'musical' of today); the tunes were mostly folksongs with new, bitingly funny words. *The Beggar's Opera* was first put on in 1728 and quite stole the audiences from Handel's Italian operas. It ran for years and years and its characters like Macheath and Lucy Lockit have almost become part of English folklore; but it had no real successors.

In Italy comic opera was known as *opera buffa* and developed from short farcical interludes that were played between the acts of serious operas—the audiences must have been glad of some light relief! These Italian works were all sung, much of the music being a new, very fast recitative that was only possible with a language like Italian. The most famous *opere buffe* are those of the Austrian Wolfgang Amadeus Mozart, above all *The Marriage of Figaro*. This was a great success when first produced in Vienna in 1786. The plot poked fun at the aristocracy; and it was said that within days of the first performance even errand boys were running around the streets whistling Mozart's tunes. Mozart followed this up with *Don Giovanni*, inspired by the sinful life of the legendary seducer Don Juan. This, too, was all the rage, but, alas, these wonderful operas did not make Mozart's fortune. The true depth and beauty of his music was not fully appreciated until well after his death. Amazing as it may seem to us, Mozart's music was considered too elaborate by his contemporaries; the Emperor of Austria told him after the premiere of his German opera *The Abduction from the Seraglio*, 'Too many notes, my dear Mozart, too many notes'. However, Mozart's marvellous achievement in his operas is not purely musical, but is his ability to make us believe in his characters and the way they behave. Gone is the stiffness of the remote characters and artificial conventions of Handel's operas. Mozart's music can make us believe even in an unlikely pantomime story like *The Magic Flute*.

Not that the singer's importance was entirely forgotten. Mozart knew that audiences came to the

Baritone Thomas Allen as Papageno the birdcatcher in *The Magic Flute*. The opera's librettist, Emmanuel Schikaneder, created the part for himself

opera to hear good singing; but he also knew where to put elaborate vocal display to enhance the story rather than bring it to a halt. Furthermore, he wrote his parts for particular singers and designed the music so that they would sound their best even in simple music. Long after the original singers have been forgotten, though, his operas have survived the test of time and are well loved wherever opera is heard.

## Bel Canto

The Italian people's great natural love of singing led, in the late eighteenth and early nineteenth centuries, to a special type of operatic performance

known, quite simply, as *bel canto*, or 'beautiful song'. Vincenzo Bellini and Gaetano Donizetti were two composers who understood perfectly how to shape arias to give singers the very best opportunities to display the beautiful tone of their voices, and sometimes also their brilliant vocal agility. Gioacchino Rossini, their contemporary, knew the *bel canto* style equally well; and he extracted the very last ounce of technique from singers by making them jump through the most tricky vocal hoops. He could keep up a fantastic work rate and produced thirty-six operas in nineteen years. The one most regularly performed today is *The Barber of Seville*, a hilarious comic opera with many of the same characters already featured in Mozart's *Figaro*. Rossini's music, even more than Mozart's, is full of humour and often seems positively to bubble over with pure fun. For the singers, though, it is very challenging and requires perfect technical control, particularly in the frequent *fioriture* or ornaments (fast notes that fill in between the notes of a tune). Rossini's last and grandest opera was *William Tell*, written for Paris and more serious in style than his Italian operas. Its thrilling overture is very familiar, though we do not

Joan Sutherland, soprano, in the title role of Bellini's opera *Norma*. She is a Druid priestess in Roman Gaul

21

often hear the rest of the music, as the plot requires many elaborate—and expensive—changes of scene.

## Giuseppe Verdi

Greatest of all names in Italian opera, Verdi never forgot that audiences went to the theatre to hear memorable music beautifully sung, and his tunes—choruses, ensembles and arias—were soon echoing round the world. Verdi's long and marvellously fruitful career, though, was concerned with much more than that. As he matured he was more and more determined to make music and plot equal partners, rather than using the words simply as a vehicle for the music. In this continuous quest for a true marriage between music and drama Verdi had to contend with his singers. A lot of them still cared for nothing but themselves, and used all kinds of tricks to further their own ends. One practice was to pay groups of people to attend their performances and lead the applause. These 'claques', as they were called, could be as well rehearsed as the people on stage, knowing precisely when to applaud, and when to stop, so that their star secured the most encores and curtain calls! Encores (singing a whole piece twice) were another frustration for Verdi, as he strove for better drama in his operas. But Italian audiences loved them, especially if the aria to be encored was full of tricky runs and leaps, or ended on a high, sustained note. For them it was rather like getting an acrobat or tightrope artist to go through his act again, and waiting to see if he would slip!

Nothing, however, could come between Verdi and the Italian people during the turbulent years of the nineteenth century when the country was fighting for political unity and independence. The people found expressed in many of his rousing choruses and arias their own desire for freedom; and they even took his own name as a patriotic slogan, for the letters V-E-R-D-I also stood for *Viva Emmanuale, re d'Italia* ('Long live Emmanuel, king of Italy'). And however much Verdi may sometimes have wished to topple the singers from their pedestals, they were all soon enough clamouring to be heard in *Rigoletto, La Traviata, Il Trovatore, Don Carlos, Aida, Otello* and his other famous operas.

Verdi at the age of 84.
He was already over 80
when he finished his
last opera, *Falstaff*,
which bubbles over
with good humour

Verdi fretted at the self-indulgence of singers, and at the conventions of opera that stood in the way of real dramatic action. Many operatic composers had felt the same kind of frustration. In the eighteenth century the composer Christoph Willibald Gluck had made his case for treating words and music with equal consideration in the interest of good drama. For Verdi's German contemporary, Richard Wagner, however, mere reform was hardly enough. He had the vision of an entirely new kind of performing art that rolled music, poety and drama into one. *Gesamtkunstwerke*, or 'whole art work', was his ponderous German term for it, and there would be no room for prima donnas.

## Richard Wagner

Wagner took as his starting point a tradition of German opera that was quite different from either Italian serious or comic opera, or from French opera-ballet. This went back to a form of stage entertainment, very popular in Vienna, called *Singspiel* (song play). It was a kind of pantomime, with spoken parts interspersed with songs and other vocal ensembles. It was a famous Viennese *Singspiel* artist, Emmanuel Schikaneder, who commissioned Mozart to compose *The Magic Flute*; and in the first production of this most extraordinary opera, Schikaneder played the pantomime part of Papageno the birdcatcher. Ludwig van Beethoven's only opera, *Fidelio*, could hardly be described as *Singspiel*, for it has a serious revolutionary theme of freedom from political tyranny; but it does have spoken words between the musical numbers. Carl Maria von Weber also added to this distinctive type of German opera, notably with *Der Freischütz* (*The Marksman*), a tale of German peasant life and of the supernatural that the Germans themselves have always loved.

Wagner built upon this foundation with *The Flying Dutchman*, *Tannhäuser* and *Lohengrin*. Each takes a big step forward in dramatic power and in the balance between words and music; but each was still only a step towards his ideal 'whole art work'. Wagner's operas owe much to the *Singspiel* tradition—though he did not use spoken dialogue to break up the musical numbers. In fact, as he developed his own style he gradually abandoned the old distinction between speech-like music (recitative) and tuneful music (aria), and instead created a continuous tapestry of sound in which the singers declaim their lines simply as one more thread. Often the most important tunes are played by the orchestra, not sung, and there are sometimes several going on at once! Wagner's operas are very long—up to five hours—and many people find them difficult to listen to at first. But there are many operagoers who prefer his music to any other composer's. Perhaps his most approachable opera is *The Mastersingers of Nuremberg*, his only comedy.

It took Wagner twenty-five years to realize his dream in the huge cycle of four operas, or 'music dramas' as he called them, known as *The Ring of the Nibelungs*. The text of *The Ring*, which Wagner finished writing before starting on the music, is based on ancient Norse and Teutonic myths and legends—though people have since read every kind of political, philosophical and religious meaning into it. The

The Rhinemaidens swimming around their coveted gold in an early production of *The Rhinegold*, the first of the four operas, or music-dramas, comprising Wagner's *The Ring of the Nibelungs*. The effects the composer called for, from the antics of these Rhinemaidens to the Ride of the Valkyries, taxed the ingenuity of stage designers almost too far

Spanish tenor José
Carreras as Lieutenant
Pinkerton with Yasuko
Hayashi as Madam
Butterfly—Puccini's
most tender and tragic
heroine

seventeen hours of music that support this story include no conventional arias or operatic ensembles; and thus the singers are given little chance to show off their own special vocal qualities or tricks. The qualities they need are vocal power, stamina and concentration. When the various parts of *The Ring* and Wagner's other music dramas first appeared most singers took one look at the music and threw up their hands in horror. People's worst fears about what such music might do to a singer seemed confirmed when Ludwig Schnorr, the first tenor to take on the role of Tristan in *Tristan and Isolde*, died soon after the first few performances. Some years later when the already famous Nellie Melba attempted the huge role of Brunnhilde in *The Ring* she had to retire from the operatic stage for nearly a year to recover from the experience. Great Wagnerian singers, in fact, are not typical of the world of opera as a whole. They need a special kind of temperament as well as a special kind of voice. The Norwegian Kirsten Flagstad, who was perhaps the greatest of all Wagnerian sopranos, used to sit in the wings placidly knitting, until it was her turn to take the stage and pour out her voice by the hour.

## Later Opera

Verdi in Italy and Wagner in Germany dominated opera in the nineteenth century; but they had their successors. In Italy Giacomo Puccini provided singers with more beautiful soaring melodies in *La Bohème, Tosca* and *Madam Butterfly*. Ruggiero Leoncavallo, too, wrote one big success, full of singing designed to tug at the heart-strings, in *Pagliacci* ('Clowns'). In Germany Richard Strauss wrote a series of operas, the best loved being *Der Rosenkavalier* ('The Cavalier of the Rose'). The main part of the story is a rather sugary love affair that would never have appealed to Wagner. But Strauss's rich orchestration, his lush and sumptuous use of the voice (particularly the top register of the soprano) and the staying-power demanded of the singers show the strong influence of Wagner.

While Verdi and Wagner wrote operas in which music, however appealing in itself, is made to heighten the action of the plot, the French continued to indulge their love of grand spectacle and sensuality in a series of works known as 'Grand Opera'. Rossini's *William Tell* is one such work, and Hector Berlioz's *The Trojans* is another. Such pieces were rather like our film epics of today, depending for their effect on crowd scenes, grand visual effects and extravagant music. Few such operas are performed today, though those of Charles Gounod (*Faust* and *Romeo and Juliet*) remain in the repertory. Another feature of French operas was the love of exotic settings, like the Spanish background to Georges Bizet's *Carmen*, which has lived on to become one of the five or six most popular operas. At the end of the nineteenth century the influence of Wagner resulted in a new kind of opera which, rather than showing strange, foreign places, looked inside the minds of the characters by means of strange, dream-like music— such as Debussy's *Pélleas et Mélisande*.

In far-off Russia fine operas were written by Mikhail Glinka (*A Life for the Tsar*), Modest Mussorgsky (*Boris Godunov*), Tchaikovsky (*Eugene Onegin*) and Nikolai Rimsky-Korsakov (*The Golden Cockerel*). In Bohemia Bedřich Smetana filled his opera *The Bartered Bride* with the enchanting folk songs and dances of the country that he hoped would one day become independent as the new nation of Czechoslovakia. After him Leoš Janáček wrote several operas that are remarkable for the way the music follows the shape of the Czech language.

The special care that Janáček took to marry his music to the sound and character of his native tongue introduces a problem that opera lovers have argued about for a long time. Some say that the connection between the words and music as originally set by the composer is so strong that to translate the words into another language ruins the effect. Others reply that it is stupid to present an opera in a language that few of the audience can understand. Both sides have a strong case, and the argument is never likely to be resolved; and in London audiences are lucky enough to have a choice between Covent Garden, which usually puts on operas in their original language, and the English National Opera, which produces everything in English. Meanwhile, opera singers may have to learn a role in two or three languages, to

A rare picture of the first production, Moscow 1879, of Tchaikovsky's opera *Eugene Onegin*. The work is based on a poem by Alexander Pushkin, and in this scene two of the principal characters, Onegin himself and his erstwhile friend Lensky, are challenging each other to a duel

(*Opposite*)
The foyer of the Paris Opera House, as it looked soon after its opening in 1875. Opera houses were (and still are) status symbols in the life of a city—none more so than this opulent building

suit the requirements of different opera houses. This can be a very taxing business—comparable to a pianist being asked to re-learn a long piece of music with completely new fingering. Occasionally this language problem can have comic or embarrassing consequences. For singers have sometimes stepped into a role at short notice, to find that they are singing their part in one language, while the rest of the cast are holding forth in another!

People have been attacking opera as irrational, extravagant and just plain idiotic ever since it started. In addition to all its conventions and contrivances, they point to the fact that words and music move at different speeds, with sometimes ludicrous results. Thus it takes someone only a second and a half to say 'I am dying', while song could transform this into a statement that might go on for several minutes. 'I must flee!' is another familiar operatic statement that can rather lose its effect when the singer stands and repeats it at the top of his

voice for five more minutes. Good composers, though, have usually found a way round such difficulties, and many in our own time have gone on writing operas. The Austrian Alban Berg, for example, added a striking new chapter to opera history with *Wozzeck*, the harrowing story of a poor, downtrodden soldier. Benjamin Britten was the first English composer to write great operas since Henry Purcell's *Dido and Aeneas* was produced in 1689. Britten's opera *Peter Grimes* was first produced in 1945; and this powerful drama of life in a nineteenth-century Suffolk fishing village, with its strong tang of the sea, was soon being cheered in opera houses all over the world.

## Some Famous Singers

The tenor Sir Peter Pears, who first sang the part of Peter Grimes, in Benjamin Britten's opera of that name is by nature thoughtful and retiring—not the words to describe some of the illustrious singers of the past. In the last century especially, great sopranos were idolized more than any other group of people in the whole history of entertainment. They were called 'divas', meaning goddesses, and it is not surprising that this kind of adulation sometimes turned their heads.

Early in the century the most celebrated diva was the Italian Angelica Catalani. When she visited Paris, Napoleon offered her a fortune, virtually commanding her to remain in the city. She turned him down and went on to London where she earned a huge sum of money just for singing 'God Save the King'. On another occasion at the Leipzig Opera House she complained that a rug on the stage was not good enough for her to step on to and had a rare Indian scarf placed at her feet. A second Italian diva of the same period, Giuditta Pasta, had coins minted in her honour after the fashion of kings or Roman emperors. Jenny Lind was adored as the 'Swedish Nightingale'. She was a gentle, unassuming woman, but that extraordinary showman Phineas T. Barnum made her into a sensation when he engaged her for an American concert tour, soon amassing great fortunes for them both. Later a concert hall in New York was specially built for her solo recitals. Another celebrated nineteenth-century

A picture of Jenny Lind taken in later life. Quiet and retiring, Jenny was quite unlike other great singers. She stopped singing in opera because she thought it immoral, but still the crowds flocked to hear her

soprano to be fêted like a princess was Adelina Patti. She was once asked which crowned head of Europe she liked best. 'Well,' she replied after giving the matter some thought, 'the Tsar Alexander gives the best jewellery.' And at the end of one recital in St Petersburg (the old Imperial Russian capital, now Leningrad), six generals carried her up to her hotel suite of rooms in a chair bedecked with flowers, to the accompaniment of a band! In the end, she earned so much money that she could retire to a castle in Wales and build her own private opera house.

Men have never matched that kind of glamour, but the ones who came closest to it were the tenors. Most celebrated of this breed was Enrico Caruso, the poor boy from Naples whose name and voice became

A clever caricature by Enrico Caruso of himself in Leoncavallo's *Pagliacci*—the opera about a group of players whose personal dramas suddenly spill over into their play, with tragic consequences

famous the world over, partly because in the early years of this century he was one of the first great singers to make gramophone records. On one memorable occasion in 1910 he was joined on record by the Australian soprano Dame Nellie Melba, singing the love duet from Puccini's *La Bohème*. Melba was a formidable diva who could not stand competition from any other soprano. But with Caruso it was different. 'When I sing with him in *La Bohème*,' she declared, 'I always feel as if our voices have merged into one.'

Recordings may have added to the fame and fortune of Caruso and Melba, but soon enough records and then radio began to have the reverse effect by removing the air of mystery and magic that had surrounded the old time opera stars. Because they can now be whisked around the world so fast, and because of all the added exposure through radio, records, cassettes and television, opera singers have lost the glamour they once enjoyed when people might have a chance to see and hear them only once in

Dame Nellie Melba making an historic radio broadcast in 1920. Earlier she was a pioneer maker of gramophone records

34

a lifetime. Singers who have reached the very top of their profession in the last thirty or forty years—for example, Birgit Nilsson, Beverly Sills, Dame Janet Baker, Sherrill Milnes and Placido Domingo—can still be rapturously received and honoured and earn very large sums of money. But they are not the god-like figures of days gone by.

## Songs

Few individual songs have become such favourites as operatic numbers like 'The Toreador's Song' from *Carmen* or 'Your tiny hand is frozen' from *La Bohème*. Yet some of the finest vocal music has been written as songs, and there are many gifted singers who devote their careers to performing them—though they may never enjoy the limelight that comes the way of an opera star.

The history of song, in the context of our Western art music, goes back, as we have seen, almost a thousand years to the songs of the troubadours and other minstrels of the Middle Ages. A fascinating link between our century and those distant times has been provided by Carl Orff, who gathered together into his choral work *Carmina Burana* a number of medieval songs in praise of love and wine. During Renaissance and Baroque times lovely songs were written—true songs for a single voice with instrumental accompaniment, as distinct from part-songs like madrigals. They could be passionate, especially those by Italians such as Girolamo Frescobaldi and Monteverdi, whose songs are often like miniature operas. They could be filled with melancholy, as were most of the songs of the Englishman John Dowland, with their beautiful lute accompaniments. There were more marvellous songs written in the later seventeenth and eighteenth centuries. They often had a 'continuo' accompaniment—a kind of basic guideline of chords played on a keyboard instrument, as used also to guide singers through the recitative passages in Italian opera.

What we now regard as the greatest period of song writing began early in the nineteenth century. Beethoven wrote one group of songs called *An die ferne Geliebte* ('To the distant beloved'), remarkable for the way the songs are all linked to form a single

piece of music (the 'song cycle'). Literally down the road from Beethoven in Vienna was Franz Schubert, who wrote over six hundred songs. Very many of them are *strophic* in form; that is, they repeat the same tune in successive verses, like a folktune. Such songs include 'The Trout' and 'Who is Sylvia?'. Schubert's songs are marvellously adventurous and fresh in spirit. His greatest achievements were two big song cycles called *Die schöne Müllerin* ('The fair maid of the mill') and *Die Winterreise* ('The Winter Journey'), both of which express the feelings of a young man whose hopes of love have been cruelly dashed. The way Schubert relates these feelings to the natural world of woods, fields, sunshine, rain and snow, make them landmarks of Romantic music. An important element in these songs is the imaginative piano accompaniments, which set the mood of each song quite as graphically as the scenery and lighting on a stage. The German word for song is *Lied*, and Schubert's works heralded a great outpouring of *Lieder* from Robert Schumann, Johannes Brahms, Hugo Wolf, Gustav Mahler and Richard Strauss.

In one respect, many of these *Lieder* stood for the

Schubert, at the piano, trying out some of his songs with a group of friends. The composer was well liked by those who knew him, but he died at the age of 31, unknown to the world at large

37

growing sense of national identity felt by the Germans. Feelings of national pride ran high during the nineteenth and early twentieth centuries in most European countries, and composers often used song to express them. Edvard Grieg in snowy, mountainous Norway and Manuel de Falla in hot, dusty Spain based their songs firmly on the folksongs and dances of their native lands. Mussorgsky in Russia wrote some groups of songs so strong in local feeling that they seem to carry with them almost the smell of the Russian earth. In France composers were not so passionately patriotic, but there was a continuous, inspired flow of *chanson* or *mélodie* from the pens of Gabriel Fauré, Henri Duparc, Debussy, Maurice Ravel and Francis Poulenc. Across the Channel composers like Benjamin Britten, Gustav Holst and Ralph Vaughan Williams turned away from what they felt to be the empty pride of the British Empire, and expressed a love of their country through songs inspired by English folk music—or even arrangements of real folktunes. In America, Charles Ives wrote many songs, often delightfully brash and unbuttoned, about life in the New England towns and farmsteads he loved so well.

In our own century there have been some extraordinary developments in song writing. None has made a more lasting impression than a song cycle written by Arnold Schoenberg called *Pierrot lunaire* ('Moonstruck Pierrot'). It employs a revolutionary idea called *Sprechgesang* ('speech-song'), requiring the singer to make his or her voice hover halfway between speech and true song. Schoenberg thus suggested the dream-like, often nightmarish images of the songs. Such a use of the voice was at first regarded as impossible or outrageous by many singers, but since then composers have asked singers to scream, groan, grunt or do other even more unusual things with their voices—and always someone has been found who can cope.

# Sherrill Milnes
# An Opera Star Today

# 2

When you see Sherrill Milnes on the stage as one of
the heroic characters in a Verdi opera, you feel
straightaway that he was born to be a great singer.
With his tall, athletic figure and commanding
presence he can dominate any dramatic scene, and he
has the voice to match his appearance—a powerful,
rich and varied baritone. His tone may be dark and
heavy for a moment of high drama, or soft and light
for a love duet, but in either case it will wing across to
every member of the audience even in the biggest
opera house. You might feel that opera was his one
ambition from his early days—but here you would be
quite wrong. As a schoolboy he set his mind on a
musical career, but he was in his early twenties
before he began to consider opera as a serious
possibility. Once he had started, however, there was
no stopping him, so it did not take him long to become
one of the small group of international stars sought
by every opera house and record company.

'I was brought up to milk cows and to have an
interest in music,' is his own description of his
boyhood. This odd combination was due to family
circumstances in Downers Grove near Chicago,
where his father ran a dairy farm and his mother was
a piano teacher and choirmaster. 'I learned to play
the piano when I was about six,' he recalls, ' and then
the violin a year later. Like most kids, I wasn't crazy
about lessons or practising, so I used to play around

Sherrill Milnes at home with his wife Nancy and son Shawn

until I realized the next lesson was looming, then I'd work on my exercises really hard to catch up. My father had a collection of records, mostly of the old opera singers like Caruso, and I enjoyed listening to these, though it wasn't with any thought of becoming a singer myself. Music fascinated me, however, and I tried quite a few instruments, clarinet, tuba and double bass, with the violin my favorite and the one I stayed with longest.'

Music was certainly uppermost in his mind when he went on to university, because he chose to take a music degree. 'My idea then,' he explains, 'was to become a teacher, but those studies have certainly come in very useful throughout my singing career, as all musical knowledge and experience helps you as a performer. While I was at college I also started to perform in public, as a violinist and as a singer with a dance band, and that was useful experience too. Finally I took singing lessons as well, though I didn't reckon my voice was very good. I still have some tapes I made when I was about nineteen, and the sound I produced then is nothing like the baritone sound that came later. I hate admitting it, but my voice was like a nasal tenor with no top notes.'

It can't really have been as bad as that, because he was soon taken into the chorus of the Chicago

Symphony Orchestra. A lot of singers shy away from
this kind of work if they have ambitions of becoming
a soloist, but Milnes takes a different view. 'I learned
a great deal from that experience, because the orchestra had a marvellous conductor, Fritz Reiner,
who was an absolute perfectionist. He ruled with an
iron hand, but he made you work really hard and
improve all the time. I also discovered what it was
like to sing from behind the orchestra, which is what
you have to do as an opera singer on the stage. I was
astonished at first by the sheer volume of sound made
by the orchestra, and when I was eventually asked to
sing a solo I thought, "You must be kidding. How can
anybody get his voice over all that sound from eighty
or so players?" But all those performances as a
member of the chorus had helped teach me how to do
it, even though I hadn't been aware of it at the time.'

By then he had finished his college studies and
taken up teaching, the career he had always wanted.
'I had a variety of pupils, some for singing lessons and
others for the various instruments I played. That
made me a living, and I was free to look around for
opportunities to continue singing myself. I was
always a good job-hustler, so I sang solos in churches
and synagogues, and found my feet on the stage in
amateur opera productions. That was valuable,
because when you take part as a soloist with others of
similar age and experience you are able to judge how
you compare, whether they are better than you or
you are better than them. When you find yourself
coming out on top you feel you are making progress. I
had an unexpected stroke of luck when I was offered
two television commercials. . . . They made a lot of
money, and my voice was heard on US television all
through the sixties.'

Looking back on those days, Milnes makes them
sound quite fun, but they don't add up to the usual
grounding for an opera star. 'Most singers at that
age,' he admits, 'are full of big ideas, like the New
York Metropolitan is just up the road and La Scala,
Milan, is just around the corner. I didn't have that
kind of ambition when I was in my early to middle
twenties. I was happy being a teacher, because I
loved the work, and the pleasure I got from singing in
churches and women's luncheon clubs was a very

41

enjoyable bonus. The idea that I might be a professional opera singer only came when I passed an
audition for Boris Goldovsky, who ran a famous
touring company. Even then I was not taken into the
company straightaway, but invited to Goldovsky's
opera workshop at Tanglewood. I was twenty-four at
the time and had never even heard of Tanglewood, so
I felt I had failed this audition like several others
before it. But once I started at the workshop I realized
how valuable it would be, for I was able to get my
teeth into about fifteen important roles under expert
supervision. A year later I went out on tour with the
company, and over the next five years I sang about
three hundred performances in a dozen different
roles, travelling over a hundred thousand miles by
bus.'

The tours soon provided dividends in the form of
invitations to sing with various regional opera
companies as well. Now he had to face up to a
decision whether or not to burn his boats and go all
out for the big time. 'I hesitated for quite a while,
because I've always been very cautious and practical. I'd always gone to auditions determined to do my
best, and if I was considered good enough for the job I
was only too grateful to accept it, but I never
expected to become a star. Finally I won the
American Opera Auditions in 1964, which brought
me my New York debut at the City Opera later that
year, as Valentin in *Faust*. Even then I didn't burn
my boats; I continued to live at Downers Grove for
another year, moving to New York only when I was
given a three-year contract with the Metropolitan
Opera there.'

It was his successful audition for the Metropolitan,
arguably the world's leading opera house, which
paved the way to stardom. He made his debut there,
again as Valentin, the same night as Montserrat
Caballé, already established as a prima donna, was
singing. 'This was a calculated risk on my part,' he
admits, 'because I knew on the one hand that her
appearance would ensure the fullest press coverage,
while on the other hand there was the danger that I
might be overlooked in the rush to write about *her*
debut. Fortunately the risk paid off, and I was asked
to sing many more performances than my contract

had stipulated.'

He was then thirty, so all this sounds like a long haul to the top. But opera demands more training than most performing arts, so in fact he 'arrived' at an ideal time in his career. 'You need to be fairly mature,' he explains, 'to make the most of your big chance when it comes along. You have to build up your voice carefully over a longish period, you need

As Macbeth—the first of Verdi's Shakespearian title roles and a favourite of Milnes'

43

to have a number of different roles under your belt before you expose yourself to the international limelight, and you must be personally mature enough to deal with the problems of a very temperamental business. Some conductors and producers, for instance, are ready to shoot down any new singer they think is too cocky, so you have to tread warily, and there is jealousy among singers. If you've reached the age of thirty, as I had, you have the maturity to handle such situations and come through.'

He was also wise enough not to be carried away by his immediate popularity with the public and acclaim by the critics, who had all been waiting for a new American baritone to arrive on the scene. 'A lot of people who are born with a talent for singing or acting believe that because they are blessed with this talent the world owes them a living. I don't think this is the case at all: we have to work on that talent, not just at the beginning but all the time. However successfully your career progresses, you have to put everything you've got into it, making sure, for instance, that you don't take on big new roles until you are really ready for them. Then you have to prove your worth at every performance. This is where being a singer is different from being a doctor or a lawyer, who are guaranteed a career once they have all the necessary degrees. You can have every imaginable musical qualification on paper, but you could still be rated zero as a singer when it comes to actual performance. You only succeed if you can deliver the goods.'

Once he had become established as the leading baritone at the Metropolitan, he began to receive invitations to sing abroad. He appeared in London in concert performances, but regards his real European debut as a new production of Verdi's *Macbeth*, in which he sang the title-role, at the Vienna State Opera in 1970. After this he became a regular guest star at Covent Garden, singing the big baritone roles in Verdi's operas, and enjoyed similar success at the Paris Opéra and La Scala in Milan. Now he can choose to sing whatever and wherever he wants, for his name guarantees full houses all over the world.

The life of the international opera star looks glamorous on the surface, with the curtain-call cheering, the milling crowd of autograph-hunters round the stage door, the jetting around the world from one capital city to the next, the fees which sound astronomical to people working in more humdrum occupations. It is certainly exciting and rewarding, but it also brings with it a lot of strain and hassle, and hotels, however grand, are impersonal places to live in for any length of time. Some singers thrive on it to such an extent that they spend their whole lives on the move, appearing in one opera in London on Monday, another in Hamburg or Vienna on Wednesday, then back to London later in the same week. For them, home is where they spend a few weeks' holiday each year.

Milnes prefers to lead a more settled life—settled, that is, so far as his career will permit. He is a highly organized person, and he runs his life along sensible lines. When he was busy establishing his reputation he used to spend seven months each year in the United States and the other five elsewhere, mainly in Europe. Now he divides up his time so that he can enjoy nine months based at his home in New York. This period involves thirty to forty performances at the Metropolitan, and also recital tours or concerts with symphony orchestras. Engagements in Chicago or San Francisco don't disrupt his family life too much, for it is always easy and quick to fly back home.

Home means life with his wife Nancy, also a singer, and their son Shawn, in a large apartment in Manhattan overlooking the Hudson River. It's a working home, of course, where he spends a good deal of time preparing new roles and constantly studying. It also includes a gym so that he can keep his body in shape as well as his voice. 'Most people don't realize that singing is a very physical activity, one which demands a high standard of fitness. Even singers with light, lyrical voices use up quite a lot of energy; in my own case, singing the heavy dramatic parts, an enormous amount of sheer physical energy is involved.'

Preparing a new role is a long process, which he starts at home several months or sometimes as much as a whole year before he will actually sing it in the opera house. 'I usually approach it musically first,

hacking it out at the piano. My eyes and ears are better than my fingers, but I do play fairly well, which is a great help in learning a new part. All singers really need to be able to play the piano, and I soon realized how useful my early music studies were going to be. After this I get down to studying the words more closely, going through the translation as well. Then there are stylistic decisions to be taken, which might mean going to a coach for advice if you're not certain about particular points. I used to need a coach at this stage in my early days, but now I have the experience to work out most matters of style for myself.

'The real drag comes when you think you know the words but find that you haven't fully memorized them and have to go back to the book over and over again. This can be a real uphill battle, until you've memorized the words so that they come automatically. And they must come automatically when you are finally in performance: you must know every word on the particular beat of the music, timed to a split second. The most difficult role in this respect is Don Giovanni, with all its rapid-fire recitatives, which you have to know in your sleep before you're ready to play it in the opera house. One great help in this whole learning process is to listen to a recording, not to hear how some other singer does your role, but to get the orchestral sweep. You can hear the music going on while you're shaving or drinking coffee, and it's registering in your memory.'

Mastering the words and the music takes the singer halfway to an understanding of the character as well, so when it comes to actual rehearsals with the director he is already quite well prepared. The rehearsal period for a new production varies slightly from one opera house to another, but both at the Metropolitan and at Covent Garden it is usually four or five weeks. These opera houses also try to have a run of several performances, from five to ten, with the same cast all the way through. Having prepared the whole production with the director and the conductor everything should run smoothly.

It is a different matter when it comes to an opera house reviving a production already in its repertory, because there are likely to be changes in the major

Relaxing in St James's Park, London

47

roles dependent on the other commitments of the individual singers. Sometimes a singer might fly in to take part in only one or two of the performances in the revival, which means that he might have only a musical rehearsal and no run-through on the staging, though he will have been sent pictures of the stage set in advance. 'When this happens to me,' Milnes adds, 'I make sure I get there with enough time to be able to check out the set before the performance, and I check again during the intervals and even before each entrance I have, so that I walk through the right door and don't fall over a table. I guess I might have entered the stage through the wrong door on occasion, but I've never done anything disastrous like walking in through a window of the set.'

This international aspect of opera makes it different from any of the other performing arts. A play or a musical, for instance, involves the same cast appearing together nightly for a period of months or sometimes years, and only after the first six months are there likely to be any major changes in the cast. The actors in a movie similarly work together as a team until it is completed. There are permanent opera companies, too, working on a repertory system, which keep their singers together for the duration of their contracts. Only in the international opera houses do artists converge from all parts of the world to take part in half a dozen performances together and then fly off to their other individual engagements.

This means that singers appear every year in several different operas, each one of which they must know perfectly by heart, word by word (in various foreign languages) and note by note. Even when they appear in a particular role for which they are especially famous, the production of the opera will be different in each opera house, so that for Milnes to sing, say, Rigoletto in four different cities will involve his adapting himself to four different stagings and probably to four different conductors who all have their own ideas about the tempi, dynamics and phrasing of the music.

Singers need to take special care of their health, and some become obsessive about it; but Milnes takes a more relaxed view. 'As I keep myself fit, I'm not scared of sitting in a draught. I don't smoke, and I don't like other people smoking around me—not because I'm a singer, but because it burns my nose. Also I make sure that I don't get involved in drinking too much at parties, especially on the Metropolitan Opera tours in the States, where you are lavishly entertained wherever you go. If you're not careful you could not only get stoned but end up with a hangover the next day, which wouldn't do your singing any good.'

This is not just a fad: as a star, he carries a heavy responsibility. 'You have a duty, not only to yourself as an artist, but to those two or three thousand people who are paying top money to come and hear you. They don't pay less for their tickets if you are below your best form, so you have to make every effort to give them their money's worth every time. The quality of performance varies from night to night because singers are human beings, not machines, but you must always do your best, which you can't do if you haven't taken care of yourself and kept in good condition.'

The day of an actual performance is the most vital time, so how does a singer prepare himself? 'I find sleep is a great friend of the throat, so I sleep in as late as I can. The actual time will vary, and nowadays I tend to wake up and feel ready to get up after less sleep than I used to need. I guess it's the result of having more experience and more confidence, also that as we get older we need less sleep. But if I'm touring, giving recitals every night or on alternate nights, I sometimes stay in bed until mid-day. Then I do some exercises, and after a couple of hours perhaps some mild vocalizing. Then I just pass the time watching television or, if I'm staying in an interesting place, I'll walk around and look at it. Later, around four o'clock, I start doing some heavier vocalizing, and then—unlike most of my colleagues—I eat as close to the performance as possible, and as much food as I can put away, steak, potatoes and salad. If I don't eat well I begin to feel weak during the performance. I don't know why this is, but I just sing better on a full stomach.'

Another crucial time comes when the performance is over. 'Even if you're fatigued, which you usually are, there's a strong feeling of tension. You worry about your performance, whether it was great, good or just so-so, and if it has been an opening night you wonder what the critics might say the next morning. So you don't want to be alone, you can't go straight back home or to the hotel and sleep. You need company and conversation, plenty to occupy your mind until the tension drops. This feeling is worse if you are giving a recital tour, singing maybe eight or nine recitals in two weeks, the same programme in a different place each time. Now that can really become a drag as well as a vocal and physical strain, because there's just you and your accompanist. With opera performances there's the advantage of having the other singers around as well.'

The actual planning of performances for a star like Milnes is quite a job in itself, for his commitments extend five years forward. 'My schedule is closed for the next four years, though in the last year of that period I can still fit in a few single recitals. Only in five years' time am I free to take the odd engagement involving a three- or four-week run of opera performances. I suppose I am one of about a dozen singers committed so far ahead. Productions involving several stars need to be planned like this so that an opera house can be sure of getting together the particular team they want. It's a very complicated process: if they are casting *Norma*, they need to settle the soprano first, then build around her, whereas if they are thinking about *Simon Boccanegra* they have to fix the baritone first, which might well mean me, and then go after the other singers, possibly some time later.'

The demand for his services is the proof of his immense success, to which his many recordings have contributed a good deal. He is featured in more than twenty complete opera sets, has several solo albums, and is making new recordings all the time to add to this already impressive list. 'They are very important to my career, because they have made me more widely known than I would have become simply by singing in the opera house. People who have no opportunities to go to the opera, or can only go very rarely, hear a singer on records and may become very keen fans. Recordings are available all over the

In this recent Covent Garden production of *Simon Boccanegra*, staged specially for Milnes, he sings the title role opposite Kiri te Kanawa

50

world, like movies, and have made me well known in countries which I've never even been to. Also, on the purely material side, they help to raise your fees wherever you go. Appearing on television is helpful too, because people see you in their homes and decide if they like you that they'll buy tickets the next time you come to their town.'

Recordings are also a great practical benefit to the artist, because he can listen to himself, judge his own performance and improve on any weaknesses he finds in it. 'When we are actually making recordings I listen very closely to the playbacks, checking for details that may need to be corrected, and I will probably listen to them when they come on to the market. Then it will probably be a long time before I play them again, and this will be when I am studying those particular works again.'

Being famous is something he has learned to handle quite easily. 'Opera stardom has certain advantages over other kinds, because it only makes a certain impact and you can still go around to restaurants and other public places without being recognized all the time. It's more difficult for anyone who is a famous star in sport, movies, pop or politics. I go out sometimes with Burt Lancaster, and there's just nowhere he can go without being recognized and having fans come over. Operagoers certainly recognize me, but opera is an entertainment with minority appeal, so singers don't have to protect themselves from whole crowds of fans. The telephone is the biggest problem: I get too many calls at home, which makes me wild if they come at the dinner hour. I follow the old midwest custom of eating early, around five-thirty or six o'clock, whereas most New Yorkers eat a couple of hours later, so people often ring at the worst possible time for me.'

Asked, as tactfully as possible, how he faces the thought of the day which comes to every singer when his voice gives out, Milnes has an easy-going reply. 'I always enjoyed teaching, so when I can no longer continue my singing career I shall be very happy to teach. I am thinking in terms of master classes, helping students of some real potential to strengthen and polish up their technique and working with them on points of interpretation, teaching them how to get more involved in music and characterization, and passing on to them what I have learned from my own experience. I hope this won't be for some time yet, though I already do give such classes if I happen to be doing a concert at a university or music school, because voices don't die all at once any more than they are born all at once. There comes a point when you have to give up certain heavy roles, another point when you may choose to restrict yourself to song recitals, but there isn't a harrowing moment when you walk off the stage at the Metropolitan and suddenly decide you will never sing anything ever again.'

He is equally clear and straightforward about the advice he would give to young singers. 'Sing anywhere and everywhere you can, regardless of money or prestige or whatever. Go out and take the best work you can get, pick up information wherever you can, talk to people who have any useful information or advice to give you. Above all, never assume that you know it all already, even though you must have some self-confidence and ego or you'd never find the drive to go on. You can learn from so many musical experiences, not just vocal ones. I remember once singing the solo in the Bach *Magnificat*, which has an introduction in which the cello plays the exact theme that the singer then takes up. Frank Miller, who was first cellist in the Chicago Symphony Orchestra and one of the best players in the world, played this introduction, and just listening to him phrasing that tune taught me more than I could have learned in a dozen singing lessons. All experience is so valuable that you should learn whatever you can, from conductors and instrumentalists as well as singing teachers, and sing as much as possible within your range at the time.' It is simple, commonsense advice, and it certainly worked for Sherrill Milnes.

# 3 Folk and Popular Music

## Folk Tradition

So far we have discussed 'art music' and 'art-songs'; that is, music conceived by one composer with much thought and in great detail. But there is another vast world of song that we may all have a hand in creating—the world of folksong. Folksongs grow out of the shared experiences of whole communities. Nobody knows for sure how most of them start, but they can spread like fire, and are sung, remembered and, though not written down, sung again by succeeding generations, at work or play. They frequently change their tunes or their words, and there are often numerous versions of the same basic song.

The themes of many folksongs crop up again and again. The mysterious forces of nature have always loomed large in people's minds. The Anglo-Saxon song about John Barleycorn celebrates the death and revival of life through the seasons of the year. In the many versions of this ancient song John Barleycorn is the symbolic figure who dies every winter, is reborn with the spring and lives on in the bodies of men and women when they eat and drink him as bread, beer or spirit. The triumph of good over evil, expressed in the many accounts of St George and the Dragon, is another ancient and recurring theme in folksongs. Such songs are ballads (songs that tell a story), and as well as being strophic in form they may have a

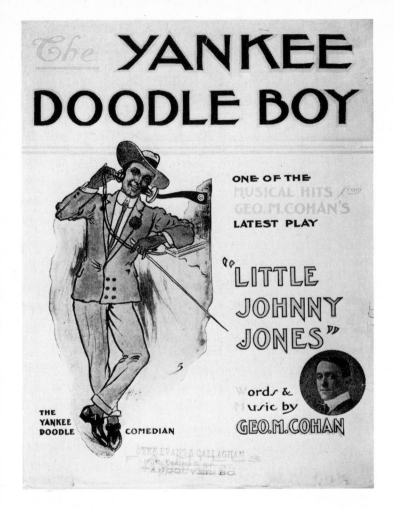

THE
YANKEE
DOODLE    COMEDIAN

An early Broadway musical, *Yankee Doodle Boy*, carried on the theme of the folksong 'Yankee Doodle'

regularly repeated refrain or chorus, since repetition has always been held to add to the force or potency of a song. Sea shanties are also noted for their persistent refrains, such as 'Hey ho, blow the man down!'; true sea shanties were working songs back in the days of sail when there was much hauling up and down of rigging, and the refrains added a cheerful note to the tough, repetitious nature of the work.

Some folksongs have their origin in particular events. The famous old song 'Yankee Doodle' originated in the American War of Independence, and became a victory song for the American colonists—though we do not know whether it was first sung by the British or the Americans. The innocent-sounding nursery rhyme 'Ring-a-ring-a-roses' has come to us from the time of The Plague. 'A pocket full of posies' refers to the bunches of herbs that people carried as protection against the Plague, and ''Tishoo, 'tishoo, we all fall down' describes the sneezing, the dreaded symptom that was followed by collapse and death. Its history shows how a folksong can completely change its meaning and character as it passes from generation to generation. Perhaps by changing a word or a note when we sing it as children, we have a hand in the long process of transformation. Scholars and composers—Cecil Sharp in England and America, Béla Bartók and Zoltán Kodály in Hungary—spent years listening to old folksongs and noting them down, fearing that they might otherwise be forgotten forever. Some of these old songs may indeed fade away. But where there are people who like to sing together—football crowds are a good example today—new folksongs are always likely to come springing up, just like the seeds of John Barleycorn.

## Popular Music

Songs have always been the heart and soul of popular music and entertainment. Popular songs can have tunes as cleverly constructed and as memorable as Schubert at his finest. They can have words as subtle as a verse by Shakespeare. The best of them also have a toughness, a durability that allows singers to push them around. For in the world of show business, most entertainers do not have refined, trained voices. When they sing a song they project their own personality; what their singing voices may be like is often of little importance, as it is the way they put the song across that really counts.

## Music Hall and Vaudeville

In the nineteenth century the big popular entertainment was music hall and vaudeville. The music hall stars based their act on songs that were virtually their personal property. In the days before record and radio, these stars would tour the halls for years on the strength of one or two favourite songs. Vesta Victoria sang 'Daddy wouldn't buy me a bow-wow' and 'There was I waiting at the church.' Marie

Edna May was a celebrated American singing star at the end of the last century. Here she is dressed for her part in the musical show *The Belle of New York*. She was the first American star to make a real hit with British audiences when the show came to London

Lloyd's all-time hit was 'My old man said follow the van' (referring to poor people who had to do a midnight flit from their homes when they couldn't pay the rent). Harry Champion sang, or delivered with enormous speed and gusto, 'Boiled beef and carrots'. Some lived in grand style; George Leybourne, famous for his songs about drink (especially 'Champagne Charlie'), used to travel between London's music halls in a carriage drawn by four white horses. The type of larger-than-life personality created by these stars has lived on into our own century in such superstars as Marlene Dietrich,

Mistinguett, the stage name of Jeanne-Marie Bourgeois. She was not an outstanding singer or dancer, but dressed in the extravagant and exotic fashion shown here, and with a big stage presence, she was enormously popular in Paris revues of the 1920s and 1930s

Maurice Chevalier and Edith Piaf.

Some popular music hall stars were black people, or people who blacked their faces. One successful song writer of the time, Stephen Foster, entranced white Americans and Europeans with his songs about the 'Swanee River' and 'The old folks at home', which painted a very sentimental and false picture of American Negro life. They are interesting to look back on, knowing as we do how black Americans were soon to turn the musical tables with the tremendous impact they made on popular music with their jazz.

## Jazz

America's black people came originally from West Africa. They had been captured, shipped across the Atlantic and sold into slavery to work on the cotton plantations of America's southern states. After the Civil War of 1861–5 they were freed from bondage, but as the war had ruined the plantations most were jobless and destitute. The one enduring feature of their lives was their folk music, the songs they sang together in the fields during the long hot days of toil, the hymns or spirituals that looked forward to the joys of heaven, and the laments on the pains and hardships of this life. They took these folksongs with them as they drifted to the towns and cities of the south in search of work. Those who found their way to the port of New Orleans began to mingle with the local creole population (people of mixed French and Latin American extraction) who had their own songs and dances. From this melting pot of races and musical cultures came the earliest forms of jazz. The lively songs and dances, springing from African rhythms, were called rags and stomps. Laments became the blues. Today we can listen to records made over sixty years ago of blues singers like Ma Rainey and Bessie Smith. They were women with no formal academic training, but with a natural sense of vocal power and feeling that no white person could hope to equal.

Many white people in America and Europe were at

Billie Holliday ('Lady Day'), one of the great black jazz singers in the tradition of Bessie Smith, though Billie's own style was rather soft and plaintive. The tough life of a jazz and dance band vocalist wore her down, and she died quite young

Britain's Ted Heath and his band in the 1950s. The vocalist, Kathy Lloyd, is out in front for her refrain, but in the days of swing it was the band that really held the stage

first shocked by this brash and sometimes crude new music; but its spirit was infectious, and the new fashionable dance styles and songs that came in at about the time of the First World War—the Charleston, the Black Bottom—had the unmistakable snap and energy of jazz. By the 1930s black American jazz had flowed into the mainstream of Western popular music, to provide the style called swing—a kind of smoothed out version of jazz rhythms and harmonies. The big swing bands played mainly for dancing, but they all had vocalists. Bing Crosby, and after him Frank Sinatra, began their careers as swing band singers ('crooners'), and records and radio soon made them household names the world over. Some of the great American song writers of the time were also much influenced by jazz, above all George Gershwin, who composed what amounted to a black jazz opera, *Porgy and Bess*.

## Rock n' Roll

When fashions in popular music changed after the Second World War, and rock n' roll came in, singers were right out in front again. In many ways, rock n' roll was a return to the earlier spirit of jazz. Its songs were like speeded up blues. It brought back

to popular music a spontaneous, personal note that had been lost beneath all the professional gloss of swing. King of rock n' roll was Elvis Presley, whose young days were spent in Memphis, Tennessee, where some of the old jazz traditions still survived. He had some instruction on how to use his voice, but it was his whole manner of performance that really mattered. On stage he made his legs and hips tremble and shake ('Elvis the Pelvis') in a way that his teenage fans found sexually suggestive—though he said he got the idea from some of the old hot gospel preachers he watched as a boy.

With the popularity of Presley and other Americans like Chuck Berry, rock n' roll spread to Europe, and in the early 1960s The Beatles began their phenomenal career in Liverpool. They were the first Europeans to make a real impression on popular music since the birth of jazz. The Beatles had a basic rock n' roll line-up, but their distinctive clothes and

Elvis Presley without his guitar, though with plenty of backing, and surrounded by rock n' rollers

61

haircuts made their performance as individual as that of Elvis Presley. They wrote many of their own songs (like medieval minstrels), in contrast to the days of swing, when singers spent a lot of time looking for songs that suited their voices and personalities. The Beatles ended up as the greatest symbol of their time—'The Swinging Sixties'.

The Beatles in America, at the height of their fame (1964). The tragically murdered John Lennon is on the right, sharing a vocal with Paul McCartney. Ringo Starr on drums, and George Harrison on guitar

## Rock and Punk

By the end of the sixties rock n' roll had given way to a much tougher kind of music that went under the general heading of rock. Rock was not 'pop' music in the sense that it was never popular with the majority of people. It was the music of young people whose attitudes towards most things, including drugs and sex, were quite different from their parents'. The differences between the generations seemed so great that people talked about a 'generation gap'. Often fierce and explosive in character, rock music could sound as though it were actually blowing a gap

62

Punk rock—
provocatively basic and
brutal. This is Johnny
Rotten and the Sex
Pistols

between the young and the rest of the community. Rock was best played in discotheques, where the loudness of the music could hypnotize the mind, and patterns of light flashed and flickered to suggest hallucinatory effects.

The greatest stars of rock have all been vocalists of a sort, though their singing may have been only a part of their performance. Fantastic clothes, outlandish hair styles and make-up, have all been essential to their act. Janis Joplin, Mick Jagger and the Rolling Stones, and Jimi Hendrix were among the biggest names in rock during the sixties and seventies. Many of them needed drink and drugs (not the first singers by any means) to induce the state of body and mind needed to perform. Some of them burned themselves up and were soon dead.

In recent years a new level of protest and dissatisfaction has been expressed in punk music. Its musical style is not radically different from the rock of the sixties, but it is usually performed crudely by young musicians with little training—a reaction, perhaps, to the exalted superstar status of the previous generation of pop musicians. The use of the voice is utterly different from what we expect in 'art music', but the raw, aggressive tones of punk are a vital part of contemporary musical expression— many would say more so than the complex and often obscure music of today's 'serious' composers.

63

Stevie Wonder, who was blind from birth, is one of the greatest exponents of progressive rock with his use of synthesizers and other electronic aids

Nevertheless, other pop and rock groups have experimented widely with synthesizers and other wonders of our electronic age, often featuring the voice, in the creation of new and sometimes quite beautiful sound effects. Their work, by contrast, has helped to close the gap that has existed for a long time now, between art music and the world of popular entertainment. They share with modern composers such as Karlheinz Stockhausen a continued fascination with the voice and what can be done with it.

(*Opposite*) Debbie Harry of Blondie in concert

# 4 Terri Balash–On the Club Circuit in America

Terri Balash is a lively, gregarious twenty-four year old who says of performing, 'it's in my blood'. She always wanted to perform. At six she urged her mother to put her into the modelling business (in those days she had golden curls and looked like Shirley Temple) and even earlier she used to march precociously into her parents' parties and announce 'Okay, I'm going to entertain now, so everybody listen'.

At five she began dancing lessons, at six she started learning the recorder, at eight the violin, and as her grandmother was a piano teacher she picked up that instrument young too. Did she ask for all these lessons, or was she pushed into them by her parents? 'I don't remember,' she answers, 'I was a child of culture; birthday presents were the ballet with grandma.' It's all so much a part of her now that how it all began does not really seem to matter.

Singing has always been there, but she did not take singing lessons until three years ago. 'I didn't take them when I was young because it's not a good idea. Just like boys', girls' voices go through a change when they grow up. But more than that, there was this fear of handing my voice over to someone else to do something with. There are good voice teachers and bad voice teachers, and a bad one can do irreparable damage. It's kind of scary.' In fact, in her teens she took a couple of private lessons one year

Terri Balash

when she was acting in an amateur production of *As You Like It* and vividly remembers the effect: 'I remember coming out after a half hour of vocalization so tight and in such pain that I knew there must be something wrong. Singing wrong will produce nodes, little nodules on your vocal chords, which sometimes can be surgically removed. But singers who sing correctly can sing for hours and hours and really never feel it. It's a muscle, the more you use it the stronger and healthier it is. But if you sing wrongly you can do a lot of damage. So I lived with that kind of fear for a long time.'

When Terri eventually took voice lessons she was astonished by the results and now believes that with the *right* teacher they are vital for a young singer. 'Singing is a very easy natural thing for me and I thought maybe he'd try to change something and I wouldn't sound like me anymore. I found instead that he didn't change my voice. It still sounded like me,

67

just better. He freed my whole voice and today I still feel the effects. I couldn't tell you what he did, but it changed my ability to sing for long periods and to get placement.' Now she feels she needs to get back into training. Opera singers study all their lives, and though she doesn't aspire to be an opera singer she realizes the great value of a trained voice.

'It's a cliché,' says Terri, 'but you sing from your diaphragm. You must breathe correctly and that requires muscle control and muscle tone and being in shape. When you see rock singers running around on stage and singing out of breath they're singing on their vocal chords. Take Janis Joplin—a classic example of a wrecked voice. She could hardly talk.'

One of the drawbacks to private lessons, however, is the cost. It's essential to go to somebody good, and the good teachers are expensive, starting at about $20 [£8.30]an hour. How often you go depends on how successful you are at practising on your own. If you can vocalize correctly at home then an hour a week may be enough. If you can't, it isn't. Ideally, Terri says she would like to take two or three lessons a week but there is the permanent lack of money.

Singing well is not just a matter of voice training. You have to be in good shape to give a performance everything. It is exhausting work and stamina is essential. Terri believes her dancing lessons have been invaluable, likewise her acting experience: 'There are singers and there are well-rounded performers. I aspire to be a well-rounded performer, not just sing songs. I think a singer is someone who can really put a song across. A singer is an actress. Like Bette Midler. Her ballads are drop-dead unbelievable.'

Starting out on her career as a singer Terri had the luck to get a part singing in *Godspell* with some of the cast from the New York company. It meant she learned the original choreography and direction. The result has been a steady source of work, as she explains, '*Godspell* is like a skill. If you have to put a *Godspell* company together fast, you want someone who knows it because it's a hard show—it's ten people on stage all of the time.' To date she has appeared in five productions of the musical and, though she swore she would never do it again, she is about to direct a sixth herself, in Toronto. Constant work like that, however, is not always as idyllic as it might seem. It can mean no movies, no plays, no dinner-parties, no holidays and at times continuous touring during which the glamour can wear a bit thin. 'The bottom line is when you're out in Oshkosh, travelling around in a bus.'

Terri gravitates more towards club singing than musical theatre now. '*Godspell* is about energy and innocence and you get to be an old, tired *Godspell* clown and it just doesn't work. It's a way to make a living, and it's safe, but I don't want to be safe.' Directing, she feels, is different, but she doesn't want to stay in musical theatre permanently. She has, after all, been working with theatres since her first job at the age of seventeen when she did *Jacques Brel* in her hometown in New Jersey for $10 [£4.00] a night. 'I'm in a transitional phase,' she says. 'I'm rehearsing with a rock group a little, but I'm finding that my heart lies in getting on the stage and being Terri the singer.' Recently she has been trying to break into the club circuit, but finds it both difficult and expensive for a young performer.

Last year she got a break when a friend suggested her as a substitute for the Boltax Club in New York where an act had been cancelled at the last minute. Terri had no act, no material, no agent, no pianist and ten days to organize the performance. Success, however, is partly talent, partly luck, but largely making the most of opportunities. Fortunately her room-mate, Carolyn, is a theatrical producer and had the time and ability to step into the role of temporary manager, so much so that she even managed to extract a small singing fee from the club. This is rare for a young performer as so many singers are looking for showcases for their talent in New York and most will appear willingly without pay just for the chance of being heard. Terri and Carolyn put the act together in nine days but found it very expensive. 'It's exorbitant when you have to pay to get somebody to play for you,' explains Terri. Musicians must be paid for rehearsal as well as performance time, invitations must be sent out, mailing shots paid for, and then the young singer has to buy something special to wear. Expenses for the show came to about $600 [£250], and

Terri sings in *Godspell*, a musical she has performed many times

even then Terri got away relatively cheaply because the act only involved herself and a piano, and the pianist did not have to write any charts for the accompaniment (usually an added expense that can cost $1000 [£400] if several instruments are involved). Since the Boltax, Terri has appeared at the Fives Club, also in New York, but still owes Carolyn $300 [£125] from the Boltax appearance.

Financing your own act is not the only way to break into the club circuit. An alternative would be to try to perform enough in Broadway, or anywhere you can make a reputation, and hope to attract audiences to club dates. From the Boltax to the Fives Club, for example, Terri found she had doubled the audience, and says with pleasure 'People would come up and say "would you put us on your mailing list,

because we want to be there next time." It blows my mind.'

Her plans for the future include auditioning for a Broadway show, or getting a band together or trying to get into recording or commercials. Of her career she says, 'It's a business, it's a job', but is determined that she'll enjoy it. 'I can't justify going to nine to five jobs just because you feel you have to. It's your life and you'd better enjoy it while you're here. It's too easy to wake up ten, twenty, thirty years later and say—where did the time go, I was doing something I hated.' Not that Terri has any illusions about the realities of the business, as she says: 'I love recording and that's where I hope I'm headed. But if you're gonna cut an album or go on the road six or eight months or whatever, that's it, you know what you

71

give up—you give up your life. You don't get to hang around your apartment in your blue jeans anymore.' The difficult decisions, however, are the professional ones.

Whether to invest two to five years, or however many years it takes to get to a Broadway show so that she can do what she wants to afterwards. Whether to concentrate on advertising work, which is less arduous but means dropping something else. 'Commercial work is fun, it's relatively easy and it's great bucks, but it means spending your energies and I would have to put other things on hold.' She knows for certain, though, that she cannot do all these things: 'I need to focus my energy. If I'm going to go for a Broadway show, I need to go to every audition. I can't diffuse now. I need to focus in on something, to try and get in touch with what I want.'

Her cabaret singing spot has opened a whole new world to her, and she thinks it's the way she would like to develop. 'I'm just starting to find out that I think my vocal tendency is going to easy-going middle of the road rock. My voice is even changing; it's getting into a more contemporary sound.' In her shows at the Boltax and the Fives Clubs she sang some soul, some light rock, like Melissa Manchester and some musical numbers such as a song from *Company* by Stephen Sondheim. 'My dream,' she says, 'is to sing in front of a big sound. I love that big band sound, that old Tommy Dorsey stuff.'

The kick she gets from performing, though, is her real reason for gravitating towards the club circuit and is part of her belief that singing must involve more than technique, detailed organization and being a part of the whole show machine. 'People who may have technical proficiency will stay forever singing in some little lounge because that's not what it's all about.' To Terri singing is about transforming a song by doing it in a special kind of way, and about the thrill of being alone on stage:

'Something happens to me when I get on stage. Something takes over. I am different than when I am sitting here just talking, but it's still me. You know when you're on stage and there's the footlights between you and the audience, you can't get enough applause and it's the most wonderful thing.'

# Vocal Training

5

## The Voice

The human voice is a marvellous musical instrument—the only living instrument there is. In other instruments the sound is produced by vibrating strings or by air vibrating inside a pipe. The sounds we make in singing are produced by the vocal cords, two small membranes in part of the throat called the larynx. During normal breathing they are relaxed and open to allow the free passage of air; but when we use our voice, we tighten them and draw them together until our breath makes them vibrate. Put your finger on your Adam's apple—the front of the larynx—and speak or sing, and you will feel these vibrations. The tighter you draw the vocal cords together the faster they vibrate and the higher the note produced.

When a boy reaches puberty—usually between twelve and fifteen—his larynx and vocal cords become larger and thicker. As a result his voice becomes deeper in pitch by as much as an octave (eight notes). A girl's voice also changes in her teens, becoming a little deeper and rounder, but it will not sound so different as that of a boy once it has 'broken'.

The sounds produced by our vocal cords are really quite feeble, lacking volume, tone and character. What gives our voice strength and individuality is the rest of our body. The violin, flute and trumpet

The Vienna Boys Choir in performance. This world famous choir is made up of young male singers whose voices have not yet broken

sound quite different because of their shape and the materials they are made from. In each case, the whole instrument resonates, amplifying and shaping the tone. Similarly, our chest, throat and head take up the vibrations of the vocal cords, giving them strength and volume; while the spaces inside the 'tunnel' of throat and nose, and the 'dome' of the mouth, lend our voice tone and quality that will make it as instantly recognizable as our appearance. Even the sinus cavities near the eyes, and also our teeth, will have their effect. How these can affect our voice is easily demonstrated when we are suffering from a cold. Swollen membranes in the nose, sinus and throat, or the after-effects of catarrh, will change its tone, as we all know.

There are two very big differences between the voice and other instruments. Firstly, while many different players may take turns at the same piano or violin, only we ourselves can 'play' our own voice. Secondly, whereas the instrumentalist can hear how his playing sounds to other people, we can never directly hear our own voices as others hear us. We hear each other's voices via sound waves conducted through the air, but we hear our own voice largely from inside. We are surprised when first we listen to ourselves on a tape recorder. 'Do I really sound like that?' is the usual reaction. It can come as quite a shock!

Of course, we can change our own voice, for example, by constricting the throat muscles, or by directing more air out through the nose than through the mouth. Impersonators and ventriloquists change their voices beyond all recognition. In normal speech we all learn to use our voice differently, depending upon our upbringing. A French child uses the throat muscles quite differently from an English child, because of pronunciation differences between their two languages. And within English itself, think of the different voices of a London cockney, an Australian and someone from Texas. Each has the unique voice they were born with, though stamped with the features of a particular accent.

Great differences also exist in the way that people use their voices in singing. In many parts of the East, people sing or chant partly through the nose, giving an unmistakable character to their music. In Moslem countries a distinctive type of high-pitched chant is used by the muezzin as he calls the faithful to prayer from his minaret. Again quite different is the incantation of Tibetan monks, in which they use their voices in the lowest possible register—a strange, almost uncanny sound. In the West, we are taught to open our mouths wide when we sing, and let the sound come flooding up from our throat. Compare the dark, subterranean growl of those Tibetan monks with the operatic tenor or soprano who can sustain a note with such power that they can shatter a glass or crack a mirror with the strength of the sound.

Above all, singing should be a joy. It is marvellous physical exercise which also releases the emotions. There are millions of people trapped in boring jobs and other routines. Most would feel better if they learnt to stand up, take a good deep breath, open their mouths, and sing!

## What Voice am I?

In opera and other kinds of vocal music, the first thing most people want to know about a singer is whether he or she has a high voice or a low voice. They may talk about a singer's *tessitura* (Italian for 'texture'), which refers to the normal range of notes the voice can encompass. But people interested in singing speak much more often about singers as

75

Maria Callas, soprano, in the title role of Puccini's *Tosca*. This part—of a singer caught up in political intrigue and corruption— inspired some of her finest dramatic performances

sopranos, altos, tenors or basses.

Soprano is the name given to a woman who can sing high notes. A woman with a somewhat deeper-pitched voice is classed as a contralto. Among men, tenor is the name for those with the highest normal voices. By contrast, a man with a deep voice is a bass. In addition to these four basic divisions of the voice, there are two other important categories, based on *tessitura*. A woman whose voice is most naturally pitched somewhere between soprano and contralto is known as a mezzo-soprano. A man whose voice is similarly pitched somewhere between tenor and bass is a baritone.

Boys' voices are classed differently. High ones are called treble, lower ones are alto. There are also adult men who have developed their voices to sing exceptionally high, usually in falsetto, and they are called counter-tenors. Today they might sometimes take parts originally written for true castrati; but there were composers, notably Purcell, who wrote songs specially for normal men with these unusually

76

Luciano Pavarotti, one of today's opera superstars, in the dramatic tenor role of Enzo Grimaldo from Ponchielli's *La Gioconda*

high voices. This is the music that counter-tenors such as Alfred Deller and James Bowman have done so much to revive in recent years.

In opera consideration of a singer's voice goes far beyond matters of pitch. The tone or 'colour' of the voice, and its ability either to tackle rapid runs and other vocal gymnastics, or to keep its strength and character through a long and arduous part, are equally important. We speak of *lyric* singers, those with a light-toned and flexible type of voice; and of *dramatic* singers, whose voices have an altogether bigger sound. There are several other special names. A *coloratura* soprano is one who can sing exceptionally high notes and also sing with great agility. Australian Joan Sutherland, who rose to fame singing Donizetti's *Lucia di Lammermoor*, is one of the finest such sopranos. A coloratura soprano of an earlier age who must have possessed a pheno-

Hans Hotter, the German bass-baritone, considered by many the greatest interpreter of the part of Wotan, Chief of the Gods, in Wagner's *The Ring of the Nibelungs*

menal voice was Mozart's sister-in-law Josephine Hofer. It was for her that he wrote the part of the vengeful Queen of the Night in *The Magic Flute*—a part that will take its own revenge on any poor singer not quite up to its frightening leaps and very high runs. A *tenore robusto* is one who can sing such taxing and powerful roles in Italian opera as Verdi's Otello. In Germany a tenor with a really big voice, capable of taking on the great Wagnerian roles of Lohengrin, Siegfried, Tristan and Parsifal, is called a *Helden-tenor* ('Heroic tenor'). The Dane Lauritz Melchior was one of the finest of these.

Temperament can also help to decide what parts within his or her vocal range are most suitable for a singer. The wonderfully dramatic baritone role of Baron Scarpia, the villainous chief of police in Puccini's *Tosca* (one of Tito Gobbi's most celebrated parts), needs a quite different approach from Mozart's callous, cynical Don Giovanni. The bass who can bring the right solemnity to the part of

Sarastro, the High Priest in *The Magic Flute*, may not feel so happy singing Osmin, the comically fat keeper of the harem in *The Abduction from the Seraglio*, or old and foolish Dr Bartolo in Rossini's *The Barber of Seville*.

## Learning to Sing

The first big question facing young singers, whatever their ambitions, is when to start serious training and study. The coloratura soprano Adelina Patti could apparently sing arias at the age of seven, and made her professional debut at sixteen. But she was unique; most girls who tried to do the same might ruin their voices forever. Sixteen or seventeen is a good age for a female singer to begin serious musical training; that is, when the girl has passed puberty. For young men the question is complicated by the breaking of the voice. Famous singers have claimed to have made an easy transition from boyhood treble or alto to adult tenor, baritone or bass, and never stopped singing at all. Again, they are exceptional. Normally, as soon as a choirmaster or other tutor detects the break in a boy's voice, usually at about the age of thirteen or fourteen, he will stop him singing for the next three or four years. This could be the end of the boy's singing career. There is no guarantee that a boy who sings like an angel will grow up to sing like Caruso. Others who have quite unremarkable voices as boys may finally emerge, like butterflies from a chrysalis, as splendid young tenors or baritones.

Finding the right teacher is tremendously important, since teaching singing is in some ways more difficult than any other kind of musical tuition. The voice is the most complex of instruments, not only in the way it works physically, but also because it is part of a person with variable feelings and moods. At the purely physical level it may take a teacher a long time just to get his pupil to breathe properly—to make correct use of the diaphragm, conserve air in order to use 'minimum energy for maximum effect'. Then the singer must control and project the voice, and focus it upon some invisible point a little way beyond nose and eyes—an area known to many singers as the 'mask'.

Only then begins the business of assessing the young singer's true qualities and potential. Many young people are quite uncertain about such things, even though it's their own voice right there inside them. They need the opinion of their teacher, who may hear in their voice, or see in their delivery, qualities they themselves are unaware of. Even over such a fundamental matter as *tessitura*, a singer often needs guidance. A perceptive teacher, for example, may advise a budding young mezzo-soprano that with time and training she will blossom forth as a fully-fledged soprano. At one time teachers had to rely entirely on their ears and general observation when making such critical judgements. Today, if they are in any way doubtful about the quality or condition of a pupil's voice, they can have the larynx and vocal cords medically examined with the aid of such instruments as the laryngoscope, which gives them an actual picture of the vocal cords.

A singing teacher has special obstacles to overcome. He cannot demonstrate on his pupil's voice as a piano teacher can push his student off the stool and

The much-loved baritone Tito Gobbi passes on his experience during a master class in Florence

say, 'not like that, like this'. He must listen patiently and be very clear about the instruction he gives, because it is entirely up to the pupil actually to correct faults. Another problem for the teacher is that while the piano, violin or other man-made instrument is covered up or put safely back in its case after use, the singer has to go on using his or her instrument in everyday speech. And while all musical instruments are affected by cold, heat and humidity, none is as vulnerable as the human voice. Colds, sore throats and catarrh are the singer's special nightmare.

With so many things that can go wrong, singing teachers are usually very cautious about letting young students practise on their own. Piano students may safely be left to practise scales and other exercises, because they can *see* as well as *hear* when they play a wrong note. Inexperienced singers, on the other hand, may not detect for themselves when they are doing something wrong, so making their teacher's task more difficult when it comes to correcting the error. A good teacher watches as well as listens, especially during the first weeks of training, so that he may nip in the bud such common faults as frowning, staring or singing with a stiff open jaw. These are usually signs of nervousness, and need to be eliminated. A singer is not going to be very convincing if he is singing the words 'I love you', while the signs of stress on his face make him look as though he is saying, 'I'd like to kill you, you swine!' Singing, like dancing, is an art, not a sport, and should appear as effortless and natural as possible.

## Coping with the Words
How to pronounce and enunciate words is, of course, a most important part of a singer's training. As the famous eighteenth-century Italian singing teacher Pier Francesco Tosi said: 'Without good pronunciation the singer robs the audience of an important part of the charm which words give the songs. If the words are not distinctly spoken, the audience finds no difference between the human voice and the sound of an instrument such as a horn or an oboe. Singers should not forget that they have words which elevate them above instrumentalists.'

English baritone John
Shirley-Quirk taking a
master class for
advanced students at
the school founded by
Benjamin Britten and
Sir Peter Pears at
Snape in Suffolk

The task for the singer is to find an accommodation
between the shaping of throat and mouth for notes of
varying pitch, and for words. A great deal depends
upon the language being sung, and many singers are
at their happiest when they have Italian to sing. Its
vowels and consonants alike are clear and bright,
like the sunny Italian sky. Watch Italians talking
together and see how most of them positively relish
their speech, especially those splendid 'r' sounds,
rolling off the tip of the tongue. Then listen to the
Duke of Mantua's song from Verdi's *Rigoletto*—best-
known of all operatic arias—and to the way the dry,
clear vowels and consonants ride lightly above the
melody: 'La donna è mobile, Qual piuma al vento . . .'
('Woman is fickle, like a feather on the wind'). Such a
language, many think, is already halfway to being
music, and reaches out a welcoming hand to the
singer.

Consider next the English language, clouded with
its many diphthongs (mixtures of vowel sounds such
as *coin*, *loud*) and combinations of consonants (e.g.,
*thick*). English may be the richest language in terms

of its vocabulary, but it can be very difficult to sing, because the voice often has to hover between sounds that have no clear and precise beginning or end. The problem is not helped by the way that many British— and American—people speak, in a rather pinched and tight-lipped way, without ever properly opening their mouths. Perhaps it is no coincidence that some of the finest English-speaking singers—Sir Geraint Evans, Gwyneth Jones, Joan Sutherland, Yvonne Minton, Paul Robeson, Grace Bumbry, Leontyne Price—have been Welsh, Australian or black American; people who are far more open in their speech than the true-blue Englishman.

French can present difficulties to a singer, because it also has difficult combinations of vowels and consonants, not forgetting that way of pronouncing 'r'—exactly opposite to the Italian—taken right at the back of the throat. It is a very smooth and unaccented language and, if not sung with care, can sound as though the music is sliding over the words rather than going with them hand in hand. German, by contrast, can act more like a kind of verbal sandpaper, gripping the voice with its heavy, guttural inflections. Sometimes, though, German can be marvellously apt. Listen also to Schubert's highly dramatic song, 'The Erlking', and to the way accompaniment, melody and words bring out the full terror of Goethe's poem about the father and his sick child riding through the stormy night pursued by the spectre of Death—the Erlking himself. At the end of the song death strikes at the child, and so with tremendous force do the words: '*In seinen Armen das Kind war tot*' ('In his arms the child was dead'). Some singers also love Russian, knowing how majestic and dramatic it can be when sung or spoken with feeling. Even Mussorgsky's 'Song of the Flea' has a weight and grandeur that would be hard to match in any other language; while the dying words of Boris Godunov inspired him to write one of the most powerful scenes in all opera.

## Singing in Opera
Young singers who decide on an operatic career will have many new skills to learn over and above the development of the voice and correct enunciation of

words. They may decide to stay in the chorus, where nearly all aspiring opera stars begin; but if they do start taking individual roles, much very hard work lies ahead of them. Seventy or eighty years ago, prima donnas could get away with a minimum of acting. After all, they would argue, the audience had come to hear them sing, not to see them throw themselves about the stage. Some of them didn't even bother with rehearsals. The poor producer would probably just be told, 'In the first act of *La Traviata* Madame So-and-so as Violetta likes to stand there'; and that would be that. Sometimes, these formidable women of the past could suddenly take too much interest in a production. Once Dame Nellie Melba objected to a piece of scenery that was placed to one side of the stage. Lifting a heavy model tree, she carried it to the centre of the stage and had it nailed to the boards.

The days of such high-handed contempt for the producer are long past. Back in the 1930s the German producer Carl Ebert showed what could be done when teams of singers worked closely under his direction in the intimate atmosphere of the opera house at Glyndebourne in Sussex. He taught them how to observe every movement and facial expression suggested by the music, and his productions at Glyndebourne, and later at the Metropolitan Opera in New York, set new standards in operatic acting.

The new Metropolitan Opera House at Lincoln Center in New York

The Greek-born Maria Callas also showed what an opera star could achieve in terms of dramatic realism. People have criticized her singing, but all who saw her on stage agreed that her dramatic commitment made her performances unforgettable.

Today opera singers sometimes complain that the producer and designer have things too much their own way. They point out that, first and foremost, they are still singers, not actors, and that it can spoil their performance if they have to wear heavy or over-elaborate costumes that restrict their breathing, or are made to sing some difficult passage while negotiating a steep flight of steps. Nevertheless, today's opera singers rehearse their changes of expression, gestures and movements as rigorously as straight actors. Thus they claim that theirs is the most demanding job in the whole field of the performing arts. They have to learn hours of difficult music as well as the words that go with it. In performance they have to control their breathing and pace their voices in order to execute particularly tricky music or to hit and sustain very high or low notes. At the same time they must be in a position to watch the conductor at critical moments in the score—and in addition to all this they are expected to observe every step and gesture taught them by the producer.

Britten was very fond of writing for children's voices, as here in *Let's Make an Opera*. There are also songs for the audience to sing in this piece

A special skill required of many singers is to keep on singing in tune even when they cannot hear their own voices properly. Opera singers often have this problem, particularly when engaged in love duets such as between Mimi and Rodolfo in *La Bohème*. Locked in each other's arms, each singer only hears the other's voice (as well as getting a good look at their tonsils). They must control their own singing by sensing in their chest and head the register or placement of their voice—something that comes only with experience. Singers who take solo parts in big choral works, or in song cycles with a big orchestral backing, also need this ability to *feel* the sound of their voice.

## Singing Songs

While opera composers specify very clearly what kind of voice they want for each part (soprano, tenor and so on), composers of songs are often quite vague on the point—probably because the singer does not have to be considered as part of a team. This gives singers plenty of scope, and also offers listeners some fascinating comparisons between renderings of the same song by, say, a tenor and a baritone. Women sing songs from Schubert's *Die schöne Müllerin*, which is all about a young man's hopeless love for a girl; while men have been known to sing Schumann's song-cycle *Frauenliebe und leben—A Woman's Love and Life*.

It is essential for the singer to find a sympathetic accompanist. The German baritone Dietrich Fischer-Dieskau's superb singing of Schubert, Schumann, Brahms and Wolf owed much to his long association with the accompanist Gerald Moore (who, of course, was the favourite accompanist for many other great singers). The French baritone Pierre Bernac was equally renowned for his renderings of the songs of Poulenc, because the composer himself was his life-long friend and accompanist. Such singers are the chamber music specialists of the world of singing. They are happy working with perhaps only one other person, and getting to the very heart of a song through the rapport they enjoy with a trusted partner.

In some respects, singers who specialize in song

Dame Janet Baker is classed as a mezzo-soprano, but in many respects she is the natural successor to the great contralto Kathleen Ferrier

Feodor Chaliapin in his most powerful role—as Mussorgsky's Boris Godunov, the tsar tortured by feelings of guilt and fear

need an even finer vocal technique than opera stars. They are placed under a musical microscope, for they are on their own. They are usually much closer to the audience than they would be in a theatre, so that every nuance both of voice and manner is quickly exposed. They have to sustain the mood of each song without the aid of costumes, scenery or lighting; and, because they usually sing in relatively small recital rooms, they must keep the tightest control over the volume of their voices—a true mark of vocal skill. What attracts singers to recital work is that their voices are not under such strain as in the opera house. They also enjoy greater artistic freedom— choosing their own programmes and even changing the pitch of a song if it suits their voice better. Few recital singers, though, would now dare to go as far as the great Russian bass Feodor Chaliapin. Before his recitals he used to distribute among the audience a numbered list of all the songs in his repertory. Then he would come on to the platform armed with a massive pile of music. A whispered consultation with his accompanist often followed, and he would announce which song he had decided to sing, calling out its number like an item on a menu!

87

## Studying Voice

There are few basses who could compete with Chaliapin's voice, but there is plenty of competition among young singers of all categories to enter the profession. In Britain, London's Guildhall School of Music and Drama has a high reputation in the field of singing, and there is always a queue of young people hoping to gain a place. Nearly everybody will have shown promise at their local school, and had some singing instruction. Entry to the Guildhall School is by audition. Naturally, voice quality comes first, but in a number of other tests candidates must show a keen musical judgment and be able to read music at sight. There are often nearly a hundred youngsters competing for the twenty or so places available at the start of a new year.

Those accepted for the three- or four-year courses leading to the School's Graduate or Associate qualifications are mostly in their late teens or early twenties. They spend a lot of time with their tutor, analyzing and improving their vocal technique, correcting any fault that crops up, and working through songs and arias, bar by bar. Relations between tutor and student are warm, friendly and relaxed, but the work rate is concentrated and hard. Then there are master classes that bring many of the students together in one of the main lecture halls. Three or four of them have specially prepared pieces, and they take it in turns to go up on to the platform and perform before a senior or visiting tutor.

Let's look in on one of these classes. Student number one, with her accompanist, makes her way on to the platform. She announces that she will sing one of Brahms's *Lieder*. Everyone listens intently while she sings the song through. It sounds good, but the tutor is not entirely happy. 'Too much vibrato on the high notes,' she says. 'Are you nervous?' The student nods anxiously. 'Nothing surprising about that,' the tutor assures her. 'But we must see what we can do about it.' She walks across the platform and feels the student's neck and throat while she sings a few test notes. 'Now you feel the back of your jaw when you sing. Go on, that's it. Do you feel the jaw itself wobbling a bit? Yes! Now try again. Let the jaw relax. Go on.'

Singing is an important part of an actor's training. Here some drama students go through their paces

The student begins the Brahms again. The tutor stops her after a few more bars. 'No, my dear. You take too sudden an intake of breath at that point. It breaks the flow of the melody. Try it so.' They begin once more. The tutor turns to the question of voice projection. 'On that note you have to send the voice away. But don't go running after it! Keep your head on your shoulders. Try it again please . . .'

Then it is student number two's turn. She has a higher *tessitura* and has chosen one of Richard Strauss' most demanding songs for high soprano. 'Very good, very musical,' the tutor congratulates her. 'But I'm not happy about your vocal colour. You had good colour on those top Cs, but seemed to lose it again as you came down. We must see why. Let's go back to the fifth bar . . .'

And so the class continues, with everyone deeply involved.

Despite all their training, and the qualifications they may have gained, young singers leaving such an institution as the Guildhall School are unlikely to walk straight into steady, well paid work. Many of them will find they have to take other part-time jobs, while they try to get their name and voice more widely known. Some might do session work, providing the musical backing for television or radio commercials— at least that brings in some money!

Sir Peter Pears discussing a technical point with a student at the school at Snape in Suffolk

The lucky few will find a place with the Royal Opera House, Covent Garden, or with the English National Opera, Welsh Opera, Kent Opera, the Scottish National Opera and other major opera companies, singing with the chorus or even taking small solo parts. They will almost certainly combine this work with studies at an even more specialized level.

The National Opera Studio in London is one excellent training ground for young opera singers. It is directed by the celebrated English bass Michael Langdon, who personally instructs pupils in stage-craft. At one typical morning session they might be rehearsing the quartet from the first act of *Fidelio*. Four voices, already superbly trained, flood the rehearsal studio with glorious sound. But their owners still have much to learn about how to move around a large stage and project themselves to an audience.

Michael Langdon tells them how to stand and move as they sing. 'Spread out,' he says at one point.

'There's always a tendency to bunch things up in one corner of a stage.' To the young soprano singing Leonora he says, 'Not too far forward. Mind you, that's a good fault. I'd rather drag you back from the footlights than have to push you forward!'

For all of them, though they are singing beautifully together, he has words of wisdom about how they should present their roles on stage. 'It's almost always better to overdo the acting than to underplay it. What may seem a bit exaggerated here in this studio has got to get across the orchestra and right to the back of a full house.' A big man himself, with a commanding presence, he tells them, 'Look as though you're in command. Don't let the music or the auditorium diminish you.'

## Professional or Amateur?

Youngsters who really feel they might have what it takes to be a professional singer—good voice, robust health, high musical intelligence, steady temperament, personality and presence—can always make a start by seeking advice from their headmaster or headmistress, or their school careers officer; or they can start the ball rolling with a few inquiries at their local library or civic centre.

For those who decide against singing as a full-time career, or may never seriously have considered it, there is still immense joy and satisfaction to be had

An operatic society getting much enjoyment from Gilbert and Sullivan's *Iolanthe*. Amateurs like these can sometimes reach high standards of performance

91

from singing as an amateur. Some amateur singers, indeed, are almost of a professional standard, and for them there are thriving operatic and choral societies glad of their talents as soloists. Though singing may not be their livelihood, they will still have to work hard and be prepared to give much free time to practice and rehearsals. Operatic societies seldom have the musical or financial resources to stage productions of grand opera. For them there are the delightful operettas of Gilbert and Sullivan, Franz Lehar, Jacques Offenbach, and the lively stage musicals of Rodgers and Hammerstein or Lerner and Loewe. These may sound light and easy compared with Wagner, Verdi or Puccini, but they are harder to do well than many people imagine. The very best amateur singers can also sometimes share a platform with professionals for the solo parts in big choral works like Handel's *Messiah* or *Israel in Egypt*, Bach's *St Matthew Passion*, Berlioz's quiet and reflective *The Childhood of Christ*, or Sir William Walton's fiery and vivid *Belshazzar's Feast*.

For those not quite up to solo standard, there are many fine choirs that abound in Britain and other parts of Europe, and in the United States. In Britain several big orchestras maintain choirs that are recruited entirely from amateurs. Naturally, to join one of these you must have a good voice, and probably be able to read music at sight; but to sing in such an ensemble is almost like being able to live two lives for the price of one. Doctors, shopkeepers, housewives, nurses and secretaries join together to sing under some of the world's most famous conductors, and often accompany the orchestra on trips abroad. The range of their music is wonderfully wide. At one concert the whole choir may join soloists and orchestra in the triumphant 'Ode to Joy' that concludes Beethoven's Ninth Symphony. At another, it may be a select group of women from the choir who, in Gustav Holst's *The Planets*, wordlessly transport us to the stars.

# Matthew Best
# On the Way Up

# 6

'Opera becomes an obsession. It's so fascinating to work in because it has so many different components,' says Matthew Best, who has just made his Covent Garden debut singing the part of the herald in Verdi's *Otello*. 'There are the singers, the orchestra, the sets, the lighting, the make-up, the costumes, all the people backstage, the acting, the special effects, even closed circuit television so that the off-stage chorus can see the conductor. A performance can be spoiled by a singer who forgets his lines or because the special effects don't work or the curtain gets stuck. It's an immensely complex thing and there's a huge fascination in being a part of it and helping it to click.'

At twenty-three Matthew is extremely young to be under contract to the Royal Opera House, Covent Garden as a junior principal, and he is clearly on the road to success, or perhaps—as he likes to put it with characteristic modesty—on the right road, at least. What is surprising is that he came to music quite late. It was not until he was twelve that he found he had any real interest in music at all, although he had played the harmonica from the age of four, which, as he says, 'suggested to my parents that there was some music in me somewhere'. At school in Sevenoaks in Kent there was an enthusiastic and talented music staff who nurtured his interest until, by his early teens, he was learning the clarinet, singing in the

Matthew Best (*left*) singing
the part of Seneca in
Monteverdi's
*L'incoronazione di
Poppea*

school choir and had started to write music regularly. His parents, while not practising musicians
themselves, had a strong interest in the subject and
were quick to recognize and encourage his gifts.

'I started singing lessons within a year and a half of
my voice breaking,' he says. In his case, the breaking
process gave him very little trouble. In a matter of
weeks he had changed from a high treble to a real
bass. There was even a brief period when he could
switch from treble to bass and back again with no
effort at all. 'I'll admit it's most unusual for anyone's
voice to break as quickly and easily as that.' For all
types of singing a good teacher is essential, although
it is not always necessary to start singing lessons as
early as Matthew. It depends largely when the adult
voice has settled. 'Some voices are suitable for opera
and some are suitable for oratorio or pop music. Some

94

people can sing successfully in many different fields. It's just that most singers, or rather most good singers, have had regular coaching of some sort. Some need it more than others.'

Matthew has had a number of teachers in his singing career so far, but undoubtedly the most influential and the most important to him was the Czech-born baritone Otakar Kraus, who died last year and of whom he says, 'he was one of the finest teachers of basses and baritones anywhere in the world. He'd sung at Covent Garden, Bayreuth, La Scala, everywhere, including a lot of first performances, Stravinsky, Britten, Walton, Tippett. Undoubtedly one of the post-war greats.' Acting on the principle that if you really want something you have got to get it yourself, Matthew wrote direct to Kraus, as he describes: 'I just said, "Your name has been recommended to me by so-and-so and I am studying at such-and-such a place and have worked on this and that and I would be extremely grateful if you could take the time to hear me with a view to giving me some lessons in the future." He wrote back and said, "Yes. Come on Monday at four o'clock." It was as simple as that.' For singing lessons in general Matthew stands by one cardinal rule that he thinks it is foolish to ignore—and his own experience and success seem to bear it out—which is that 'it's better to have a few lessons with someone who's really good than a hundred and fifty with someone round the corner who just happens to be cheap and handy.'

As well as having the good fortune to train with Otakar Kraus, Matthew also had earlier been awarded a choral scholarship to King's College, Cambridge to read music. This meant, of course, that he was a member of the famous and prestigious King's College Choir with whom he sang for three years and travelled all over England and Europe, and even as far as Japan. Choral singing is not necessarily the right training for opera, but as a musical training the choir and Cambridge proved invaluable. When he left university in 1979 he was accepted at the recently founded National Opera Studio in London, which offers a full-time course under a number of highly distinguished coaches.

While he was at Cambridge Matthew also wrote an

opera himself. *Alice* is based on Lewis Carroll's *Alice in Wonderland*, with a few incidents borrowed from *Alice Through the Looking-Glass*, which he conducted for three nights in Cambridge and then for two nights at the Jubilee Hall, Aldeburgh as part of the 1979 Festival. 'I wanted to write something big before I left Cambridge,' he says, 'because there you've got a ready-made nucleus of singers and lots of good instrumentalists.' Matthew recalls the opera with affection, and particularly the big set-piece of a wild setting of the Jabberwocky poem sung by the Queen of Hearts. He was also obviously delighted that Sir Peter Pears agreed to make a guest appearance reading the White Knight's poem at Aldeburgh.

Composition, however, does not seem to be happily compatible with a singing career. 'For me composition is a heavy intellectual exercise which needs complete devotion until the piece is finished. It means working through the night if something needs it, and you can't do that and hope to sing the next day. You can't just say, "Oh, I'll write half an hour a day"; a piece takes as long as it takes and you've got to see it through. I would like to do some more composition, but if I was to stop singing and take six months or even a year off I wouldn't be able to pay the bills! I'll try to keep it ticking along, nonetheless.'

As well as his work at the Royal Opera House, Matthew sings in concerts, as a soloist with choirs and choral societies, conducts whenever he gets the chance, and has had several invitations to perform abroad. To sing professionally on a freelance basis he believes it is essential to have an agent and sums up the reasons in a phrase: 'Contacts and contracts', though he admits that a good agent does far more than that. 'An agent is also invaluable for advice on which parts to take,' he says. 'In the end the decision is mine, as it must be, but I'll always ring up and say, "Look, I particularly want to do this, have you any objections" or alternatively, "Look, I don't know about this, what do you think?" At other times something will come up and they'll say they think it's a good idea, or that I've got enough on my plate, or that they don't like the arrangements or whatever. It's rather like having a wise uncle.'

Matthew's musical interests mainly revolve

around 'classical' music, but he's not blinkered about it. At the end of serious programmes he will sometimes sing one or two numbers out of Broadway musicals, like 'Ol' Man River' from *Showboat* or 'Some Enchanted Evening' from *South Pacific* (which was first sung by a great operatic bass, Ezio Pinza) and from a performing point of view says, 'Though they're obviously lighter than some German songs, I would never think of them as frivolous.' He has, however, a slightly ambivalent attitude to pop music. 'Basically I'm not tuned into rock music. Does Elvis count as rock? I quite like some Elvis, simply because I happen to think he was a good singer, but of nine out of ten songs on *Top of the Pops* I'll think, "Oh my God, I can't stick this". The tenth song, though, can be tremendous. I simply think one needs the same discretion with pop music that one has with classical music. Mozart succeeded when everybody in every court down the road was writing his own music— Mozart just happened to be better at it. If music's good it should last. Look at The Beatles.'

Sir Peter Pears reading the White Knight's poem from Matthew Best's opera *Alice*

Unlike any other art, music relies on performers to bring it alive. In order to perform, however, a singer must keep fit and well. Like all singers, Matthew worries about colds and throat infections. He recalls Otakar Kraus telling him that throughout his life he would have three nightmares—forgetting his part, being late for a performance, and catching cold. 'Singers are the most unsympathetic people if you've got a cold. Instead of saying, "Oh, you poor thing" we say "Get the hell out of here".' In keeping with this, a singer has to take precautions which would be regarded as neurotic in any other profession. Matthew avoids crowded buses and trains whenever he gets the chance. He illustrates this by saying, 'I'm a bit snuffly at the moment, so yesterday, when I could have taken two trains, one of which was leaving immediately and the other ten minutes later, I looked at them both and took the later one because it was less crowded. I left London with a handkerchief over my nose and inhaling things. You can do almost any other job with a cold. It just makes you feel a bit under the weather, but you can do the job. If you're a singer and you've got a cold or throat infection, you can't work. Some singers get neurotic about it and others are just very careful. I hope I can be counted as very careful.'

The best way to take care of a voice, however, is to keep as fit as possible all the time. This is a necessary part of the self-discipline that all singers must have and to which there is no alternative. 'If you get to the top it can be a very well-paid business indeed', says Matthew. 'Some of the very best singers may command extremely high fees—up to five thousand pounds [$12,000] a night—in opera. However, the pressures at that level are very great. A top opera star might find himself with three or four big performances in one week, all in different countries, and each audience hopes and expects that singer to be in very best form every night. So it's back to the hotel room after the performance for a good night's sleep before catching the plane in the morning. No parties.'

At a less exalted level Matthew finds it essential to make sure he gets plenty of sleep, eats properly balanced meals and takes a lot of exercise—in fact all things that any doctor would recommend for almost any profession, but which a singer has to follow unfalteringly. 'Singing is a tremendously physical thing. You must have strength and stamina from head to toe to cope with some of the big operatic roles. Ideally you should be as fit as an athlete.

Singing the role of Otello is like running the marathon and there are only a very few tenors who have the necessary stamina.' Matthew himself is not ready for such demanding roles, not only because he would be neither physically nor emotionally ready for them, but because at such an early age they could damage his voice: 'The thing about the human voice is that it builds in stamina as one's body builds in stamina. One can put far more pressure on it at the age of forty than one can at the age of twenty. The prime of one's singing career should come after thirty, so you have to take a very long-term view.'

Matthew, however, regards his patience as fully justified, and the fascination that he finds in the complexity of opera is matched by his appreciation of the characteristics of a good singer. 'A great singer has many assets, of which only one, though the most important, is a good voice. Patience, self-discipline, stamina, ability with languages, acting, self-confidence—all are part of a singer's make-up though few have all these qualities. Even if you don't have an outstanding voice you can still enjoy a very success-ful career, but one can always do with a bit of luck being in the right place at the right time. But I think there is really no substitute for hard work. It is very difficult to climb to the top of the tree, but it is even more difficult to stay there. I'm only on the first branch.'

Matthew has just started to find his feet in a profession that can be as risky as it is glamorous. 'Many teachers and parents feel that a singing career is too chancy and try to advise against it. You certainly need to think hard before deciding to have a bash at it. It's a very responsible job that needs dedication, but it's also tremendously exciting. It is easy to be tempted by the glamour and the bright lights, but this really is just the icing on the cake. For me the real thrill comes from the music—having the chance to bring the dots of the page to life.'

# 7 A Career in Popular Music

### Successful Entertainers

Nobody in the world of popular music has ever cared much whether a singer is a soprano, tenor or bass. If you wanted to be academic about it you could say that Bing Crosby, the popular singer with perhaps the widest appeal of all time, had a pleasing light baritone voice that deepened in pitch over the years almost to bass. What people the world over called him was the 'Old Groaner' and bought his records, or queued by the million to see his films. As a law student he sang and played in his college jazz band, then teamed up with two others to form a vocal group that was good enough to sing with the famous Paul Whiteman band. The young Harry Lillis Crosby knew some of the best jazz musicians of his day and showed he had just as sharp a sense of rhythm and of phrasing. He also listened closely to Al Jolson records, which helped him to form his style when he began singing seriously as a soloist. And he was one of the first to appreciate the importance of the then new-fangled microphone, using it almost as an extension of his own voice. In later years he said he owed much of his success to the fact that millions of others thought they could sing like him. 'It's no trick for them to believe this,' he wrote, 'because I have none of the mannerisms of the trained singer.' These modest words, in fact, are the observations of a brilliant and shrewd entertainer who assessed his own talents exactly, and stayed at the very pinnacle of show business for forty years.

Frank Sinatra was another fine natural baritone who has been praised for his beautiful flowing vocal line and compared with the old masters of the Italian *bel canto* style of singing. For the girls of the bobby-soxer generation who went faint at the sound of his young voice he became 'Swoonatra', and later everybody knew him as 'The Guv'nor'. Born in the dockyard town of Hoboken, across the Hudson river from New York City, he didn't think much about singing until at eighteen he took his girlfriend along to a local theatre to see Bing Crosby. Of Crosby he has recalled: 'He had such great ease that I thought, if he can do it that easily I don't see why I can't. That was one of the big turning points of my life.' His mother bought him a microphone and loudspeaker and he formed a vocal group. To get on radio he agreed to sing without a fee. He was always on hand

Frank Sinatra, Bing Crosby, Dean Martin—three great professionals making a record together

Frank Sinatra back in
the 1950s, looking
dreamy and casual but
wide awake to the mood
of each song

when one of the local stations needed a singer. Bandleader and trumpeter Harry James heard him one day, just when he wanted a new singer. Sinatra sang with him for several months, then moved on to the celebrated Tommy Dorsey band. Dorsey's own trombone playing was a great inspiration to him. Sinatra loved the flowing, unbroken line of Dorsey's solos and started to work on a similar vocal style. He also perfected his own microphone technique, holding the instrument a little way from himself or moving in close with the mood of the song, and turning his head deftly to snatch a breath. He made another good move when he took on George Evans as a manager. It was wartime, and millions of young men had been drafted into the services. Evans projected the youthful Sinatra as a kind of vocal boyfriend to all the young girls left behind—and soon he was the biggest teenage idol of them all.

Elvis Presley, the king of rock n' roll, came from a poor white family who moved from Mississippi to Memphis, Tennessee. When still a small boy, his parents gave him a guitar because they couldn't afford a bicycle. He learned to play by listening to blues and gospel singers on the radio, remembering their chord sequences and finding the right finger positions. As a young truck driver he paid to make a record of himself. The people in the little Memphis studio thought he had something more than the usual run of young hopefuls who paid to cut a disc. It didn't get him anywhere at first, but eventually he began to be heard on local radio stations, and public appearances followed. The girls went mad for his sulky good looks and heavy sideburns, his tight trousers and turned-up shirts, and the way he swung his guitar and shook his hips and legs. He also impressed the self-styled 'Colonel' Tom Parker, an old fairground trouper with a real showman's nose for a new sensation. Parker worked on the Presley image and soon got him appearing on television where he was described by one producer as a 'guitar-playing Marlon Brando'. Presley threw the young into ecstasies, and was hated and sneered at by most others. He probably never really understood the hysteria he created. 'If I stand still while I'm singing, I'm dead man,' he said. 'I might as well go back to

Liza Minnelli showing
all the energy and
commitment to a song
of her famous mother,
Judy Garland

drivin' a truck.' In private he was quiet and rather old-fashioned in the way he addressed older people as 'sir' and 'ma'am', dutifully did his military service, put on weight in later years and kept out of the limelight for a lot of the time, while the cult about him began to grow.

By comparison with Elvis, The Beatles looked wonderfully spruce and fresh-faced when they first hit the world's headlines in the early 1960s. In fact, under their first manager Allan Williams they had known tough times as a struggling pop group in the roughest parts of Liverpool. They played at places like the Garston Baths, known locally as the 'Blood Baths' because of the regular gang fights, and like other groups often had to make a mad dash for their van at the end of a show for fear of being beaten up by thugs who envied their way with the girls. An early member of the group, Stuart Sutcliffe, was brutally kicked in the head during such a scuffle, and not long after he left them he died. When Brian Epstein became their manager and gave them the new spick-and-span image that spoke for the 'Swinging Sixties', they were already a hardened bunch as well as a tremendously exciting new musical group.

There is a universe of difference between the crooning of Bing Crosby and other popular singers of the 1930s and the great flood tide of rock music ushered in by groups like The Beatles thirty years on. Yet Crosby, Sinatra, Presley and The Beatles (the four biggest names of successive generations) all managed to find their feet and their style in the world of popular music. None of them bothered much with written music or formal training. They played by ear, listened to others, tried out various styles, trusted their instinct and intuition, began to shape an individual style, and when the lucky breaks came along knew how to grab them with both hands. That's still basically the way of it, with one qualification. The great song stylists of the past—Ella Fitzgerald, Perry Como, Peggy Lee—usually looked to song writers to provide them with their material; while for a long time now most successful pop singers and groups—The Beatles themselves, the Rolling Stones, Johnny Cash, Bob Dylan—have created their own words and music.

## Starting Out

Today's young singers and groups nearly all start by doing a local circuit of pubs, clubs and discos, gradually widening their field as they get better known. They are constantly on the move from one date or gig to the next, snatching food and sleep when and where they can. Apart from back-up instruments, such as drums and electric guitars, most have their own amplification and probably an expensive synthesizer as well. It can be a hard routine, and those without real determination and faith in themselves will soon fall by the wayside.

For the ones who carry on, they will sooner or later want to produce a demo disc or cassette, not to

Bob Dylan listening critically to a play-back of one of his recordings. A very influential singer of the 1960s, he led the folk revival and gave voice to the feelings of the young on big issues in America such as civil rights

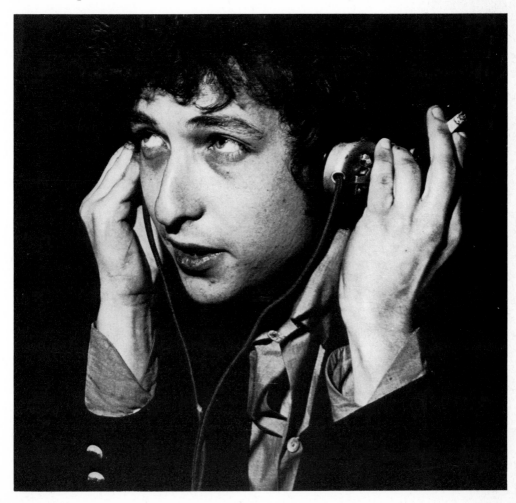

Australian Olivia Newton-John has struck a good balance between country style and MOR (Middle of the Road). She has often appeared in cabaret with Cliff Richard, another star who has always avoided extremes

market commercially but to send to record companies, and anyone else who might help to promote them, as an example of what they can do. Ten or fifteen years ago most available studios only had four-track facilities, which set a limit on what singers and musicians could do. Today 'demo' studios have eight- or even sixteen-track recording equipment, giving

108

performers the chance to get something really sophisticated on to tape. At the time of writing (1980), the cost of a day's demo recording is in the region of £100 [$230.00]. Groups or singers who mean business will make the most of this investment. They'll have several numbers lined up in advance and get them on tape in that single session. One number on its own is not really enough, however exciting it may be. People will listen and say immediately, 'Yes, I like it, but what else can they do?'

There are several other useful things singers can do. It's a good idea to accompany your disc or tape with at least one attractive photo. An invitation to future engagements is another useful gesture— recording managers like to see groups performing live. Pictures, invites to appearances, a brief but well written bit of chat about the group; this is all part of the packaging. What's on the tape or disc matters most, of course. But how it is presented can make a lot of difference when it lands on some recording manager's desk.

## Commercial Recording

The big make-or-break moment can come when a singer or a group finds the finance to produce a master disc—one that is good enough both musically and from a recording point of view to be com- mercially released. It's a big operation, probably taking several days. Usually the instrumental back- ing is recorded first, then the vocalist comes along and adds his or her voice to the existing tracks. It takes experience and nerve for a singer to stand alone in a studio with earphones on and give all he's got to a song. He should also know which medium he's aiming at. Depending on the backing and the style of singing, a record that sounds good over the air will not necessarily take so well to the massive amplification of a disco.

A pop singer or group may well start out on their own, but if they begin to be talked about and in demand, they will probably want to have a manager. As we've seen, managers have been the making of some of the biggest stars. There's another classic story of how New Zealander John Kennedy helped ex-merchant seaman Tommy Hicks to stardom, when

With Melba and Caruso, Dame Clara Butt was making records in the early years of this century— this is a 1909 advertisement. She was a contralto with a very deep voice

Bob Marley is one of the most popular singers of reggae, music of Jamaican origin which is associated with the Rastafarian religious movement

Tommy was just another Soho coffee bar entertainer back in the days of skiffle. 'I changed his name to Steele,' Kennedy says, 'because there was a steel strike on at the time, and it had a nice ring of the untouchables about it ... I had to get him talked about.' Kennedy certainly did that, and soon Tommy Steele was Britain's number one rock n' roller.

Managers don't often bring off scoops like that, but if they know their job they can still be of immense help to a singer or a group, both on their way up the ladder to success and when (and if) they make it. Singers often change or modify their style, because of what they feel is right for them or because of some change in pop music fashions. But it's not always easy for them to know whether they're doing the best thing, especially with today's proliferation of styles and trends—gospel, blues, country, western, soul, heavy metal, punk, disco, MOR (middle-of-the-road). A good manager will know all about a singer's personality, manner and voice. He will have his ear

110

Elton John, one of the most successful British pop stars in America since The Beatles, combining pop and rock styles with the kind of zestful showmanship displayed here. He began as a part-time pub pianist

close to the ground when it comes to changing trends in the pop music scene, and offer guidance in shaping and re-shaping his style. And there aren't many pop artists around who would dare to start making master discs and albums to the current tune of up to £15,000 ($35,000)—not to mention all the consequent promotion— without a manager to handle the business end of things.

## Some Words of Warning
The vast majority of pop singers and groups, it must be said, never get anywhere near the making of a

112

commercial disc. Thousands of youngsters are starting out every week, attracted by the apparent glamour of the pop star's life, and also attracted by the idea that it's a very easy and exciting way to make a lot of money. Philip Love, managing director of Eden Studios, a very successful twenty-four-track studio in London, has recorded some of today's best-known pop performers—Elvis Costello and The Attractions, Joe Jackson, Dave Edmunds and Nick Lowe of Rockpile— and he can help to put the pop music scene into perspective. 'First of all,' he says, 'it's largely a myth that most of the luck and riches fall into the laps of the young. Of course there are exceptions, but most of the successful singers I've known have often struggled for years before they've finally broken through to anything like the big time. As in other walks of life, they've reaped the rewards of hard work and hard-gained experience.'

Philip, who should know as well as anyone, also has plenty to say about the risks and pitfalls of recording. To start with, he reckons that perhaps only one singer or group in a thousand ever gets to making a master disc at all. Then there's still plenty to worry about. DJs, for example, get sent over eighty new releases every week. They don't have time to play through them all, so it's often a gamble whether a new disc will be listened to, let alone liked and played over the air. There's the risk, too, that a new group will find their record released the same week as the latest offerings from one or two international stars. Obviously the DJs and radio stations are going to have their discs at the top of the pile, and the ones underneath must wait their turn. That sort of thing can wreck a new record's chances, no matter how good it might be. 'Then,' adds Philip, 'supposing a new album or single does go well and makes the charts, there's the immediate problem of the follow-up. A couple more discs that don't take off can see a singer or a group right back at the bottom of the ladder.'

The rewards for a pop singer can be very high—the top stars earn millions— but so is the failure rate. It's a hectic, unpredictable, fickle, hard-bitten world the pop singer has chosen, and if he doesn't know that when he enters it, he'll pretty soon find out!

# Acknowledgments

The illustrations are reproduced by kind permission of the following: Roger Viollet 2; The Mansell Collection 5 (top), 12, 31; BBC Hulton Picture Library 5 (bottom), 13, 17, 18, 23, 33, 57, 58, 59, 60, 87, 102; Archiv für Kunst und Geschichte, Berlin 7, 8, 10, 25; Reproduced by gracious permission of Her Majesty the Queen 15; Clive Barda 20, 26–7, 46; Society for Cultural Relations with the USSR 30; Peter Newark's Historical Pictures 34, 35, 104–5, 108, 110; Bildarchiv Ost Nationalbibliothek, Vienna 37; Fayer 43; Zoe Dominic 51, 76; Raymond Mander and Joe Mitchenson Theatre Collection 55; Rex Features 64; Perry Schwartz 70–1; Austrian Tourist Board (Photo: O. V. W. Hubmann) 74; David Powers 77; Anthony Crickmay 78; Foto Fiorenza 80; Nigel Luckhurst 82, 86, 90, 94, 97; Spectrum Colour Library 84; Welsh National Opera 85; The Drama Studio, Ealing 89; Ilford Operatic Society 91; Aquarius Film & TV Picture Service 101, 107; Adrian Boot 111.

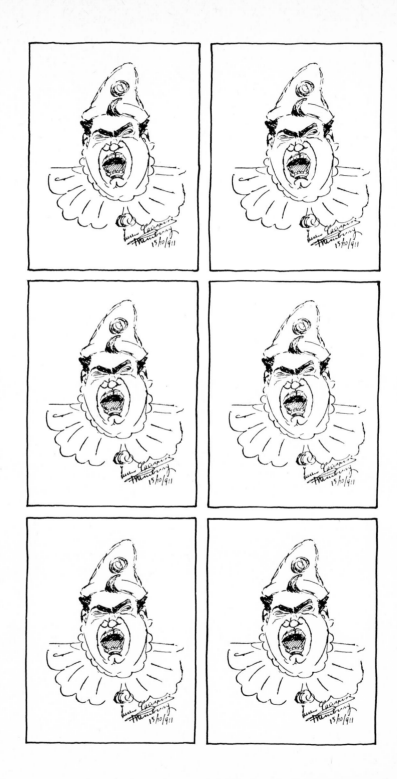

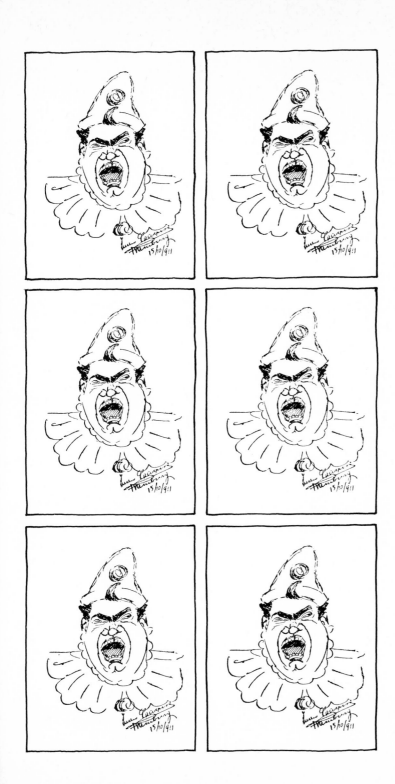